Thelma Trukabold

395 DCE69 9-68

JESUS: Man and Master

Jesus: Man and Master

MARY C. MORRISON

THE WORLD PUBLISHING COMPANY
CLEVELAND AND NEW YORK

Published by The World Publishing Company
2231 West 110th Street, Cleveland, Ohio 44102

Published simultaneously in Canada by
Nelson, Foster & Scott Ltd.

Library of Congress Catalog Card Number: 67–24757

Acknowledgments

Grateful acknowledgment is made to *The Episcopalian* for the
rights to reprint chapters 1, 3, 4, 10 and 11, © 1963, The Episcopalian, Inc.; chapter 5, © 1965, The Episcopalian, Inc.; and chapter
6, © 1966, The Episcopalian, Inc.

New Testament quotations unless otherwise indicated are from
The New English Bible: New Testament, © The Delegates of The
Oxford University Press and the Syndics of The Cambridge University Press, 1961 and are reprinted by permission. Old Testament
quotations unless otherwise designated are from the *Revised Standard Version* of the Bible, copyrighted 1946 and 1952 by the Division
of Christian Education of the National Council of Churches of
Christ in the United States of America and are also reprinted by
permission.

For
Helen Watts Chase 1880–1945
And
Helen Dana Morrison 1945–

Contents

1. Jesus as Man   1
2. Jesus as Guide   11
3. Jesus as Healer   23
4. Jesus as Teacher   33
5. Jesus as Humorist   44
6. Jesus as Disturber of the Peace   53
7. Jesus as Antagonist   62
8. Jesus as Conformist   71
9. Jesus as Organizer   80
10. Jesus as Leader   90
11. Jesus as Revealer   100
12. Jesus as Stranger   108

1

Jesus as Man

"WHAT SORT OF MAN IS THIS?" the disciples of Jesus asked. "What sort of man is this?" we ask today. What is Jesus Christ to us?

Gentle Jesus, meek and mild, a pale Galilean with a pale halo round his head?

A misty-eyed visionary? A narrow fanatic?

Merely a convenient swear word?

A dying, tortured figure, chill and gruesome, whom we have been told to love and revere, but can't?

A distant, supernatural being, a Divinity with no humanity about Him at all?

These are some of the images our culture projects. These are the images that confront many a wistful Christian today. No wonder the living image is lost; no wonder Jesus Christ is, for today's multitudes and even for many of today's disciples, the missing center of our faith—the Forgotten Man of the twentieth century.

But we can still find him. Let's look for this Forgotten Man. Let's peer behind the mighty Risen Christ of our Christian worship and meet Jesus as he comes toward us in the first three Gospels. What was his own individual way of seeing things and approaching life? What was important to him? What was he like?

In age, during the period of which we have record, he was around thirty. In any period, any culture, this may rank, at its best, as an age when the vigor of youth and the wisdom of age can meet most fruitfully—when all a man's being can fulfill itself in response and responsibility to life. We are confronted here by a man at the peak of his effectiveness, ready and able to use all his powers.

What were they, these powers?

First of all—to apply one of our prevailing values—he was fit, in a lean, hard manner that is a challenge to our use of the word. He could walk miles across hilly country; he could go for a long time without food; he thought nothing of living out in the open for days on end. He was tough. He had endurance, and he needed it—for the life he lived and for the death he died.

He was no superman, however. The thronging crowds, with their constant pressure of wants and needs, exhausted him, more than once, to a point that led him to escape into the countryside to be alone. One report gives a vivid picture of how the situation looked to some of the bystanders: "He entered a house; and once more such a crowd collected round them that they had no chance to eat. When his family heard of this, they set out to take charge of him; for people were saying that he was out of his mind" (Mark 3:20–21). Throughout the Gospels, Jesus shows a more than theoretical awareness of, and interest in, hunger, thirst, tiredness, and poverty—all the troubles of the body.

If the quality of his body was outstanding, the quality of his mind is even more interesting. He had no use whatever for dim-wittedness, and one of his less well-known parables (Luke 16:1–9) says in effect, "Who says you have to be stupid in order to be good?" In another place he said, "Be wary as serpents." His own mind had this keen, shrewd quality, and he could use it with brilliance. "They sent secret agents in the guise of honest men, to seize upon some word of his as a pretext for handing him over to the Governor. They put a question to him: 'Master, are we or are we not permitted to pay taxes to the Roman Emperor?' He saw through their trick and said, 'Show me a silver piece. Whose head does it bear, and whose inscription?' 'Caesar's,' they replied. 'Very well then,' he said, 'pay Caesar what is due to Caesar, and pay God what is due to God.' Thus their attempt to catch him failed" (Luke 20:19–26, slightly condensed). Here a slick question gets a sharp answer, one that leaves the questioners with their trap empty in their hands.

Even to such trap questions, however, his answers go beyond the merely clever. On one level they are skillful evasions; but they have their strongest existence at a far deeper one, the level of permanent truth. A frivolously exaggerated question about a woman with seven husbands leads Jesus to make thoughtful and thought-provoking statements on the nature of life after death; and a pedantic question about the Hebrew laws leads to the formulation of the great Law of Love. Jesus' mind was quick, keen, and profound.

It was also a questioning mind, with an ability to lay bare the innermost heart of a situation, and an expectation that others could and would do the same. "What do you think?" he was constantly asking; and once he exclaimed (in exasperation and sorrow), "Why can you not judge for yourselves what is the right course?" (Luke 12:57). He seems to have had more respect for human reasoning powers than many of his followers, ancient and modern—and no wonder, because he knew at first hand what the mind can do when it is honestly used, not to rationalize one's wants or defend one's possessions, but to find out the truth.

He believed that truth can be found and that the ordinary human mind, well used, can find it.

Whether his mind was an ordinary human mind, we may well wish to examine. Certainly it had many remarkable qualities. His greatest intellectual gift, the power of paradox, tends to be lost on our mathematically based civilization. We expect thought to proceed consecutively from *A* to *B*, arriving at *C*. Paradoxical thought does not work this way. The gift of paradox is primarily a humorous one and operates all at once, just as a joke makes its point all in one burst of light. Paradox pricks balloons of handsome theory, sees inconvenient contrasts, shocks comfortable platitudes out of existence, makes easy answers impossible. It says, "on the other hand . . ." and, "have you forgotten *this?*" It is very exasperating indeed—until one learns its lesson of intellectual humility, and then it becomes a great vehicle of truth. Jesus lived with paradox and made his followers live with it—all the way from the eye-opener fired at a crowd of poverty-stricken listeners: "Blessed are you that hunger now, for you shall be satisfied" (Luke 6:21, RSV), to the great central truth of all his life and teaching: "Whoever seeks to save his life will lose it; and whoever loses it will save it, and live" (Luke 17:33).

Another of his gifts is not very natural to our age: the gift of poetry. "Consider the lilies of the field"—this kind of thinking came naturally to Jesus, judging by how often his thought states itself in pictorial, poetical images. It is not a mechanical process, not at all as if he said to himself, "Now I want to say something about receptivity: what would be a good image for that?" The thought seems to come to life for him in the image itself: The Kingdom *is* the man sowing seed, the lost soul *is* the sheep wandering on the mountain.

Humor is in these images too—a camel squeezing itself

through a needle's eye; drinkers carefully straining out something as tiny as a gnat, and swallowing without a quiver something as huge as a camel; a woman turning her household upside down looking for one coin. The reverential atmosphere that surrounds Jesus in our Christian tradition tends to extinguish his humor, but enough traces have survived to show that he had it and used it.

The quality popularly known as intuition is hard to define, but we all know what it is, and we see it in operation every day. When we put together several small indications, half-consciously, and know that Johnny is coming down with a cold, or Jim is in a bad temper, or Sam is sure to have an automobile accident some day, we are using in a small way the quality that Jesus used when he knew that one person was ready to be healed; that another needed to be cut loose from his comfortable life in order to follow his best impulse; that he himself, following the course of action he was engaged in, would end his life on the cross.

He did not appear a superman in this area, however. He seems to have been intellectually a man of his age, thinking as his teachers thought, accepting the current assumptions about insanity, Old Testament history, and the authorship of the Psalms, to name a few obvious examples. He was not omniscient; he had to ask for information, like the rest of us. When someone touched him and he wanted to know who it was, he had to ask (Mark 5:30). Earthbound questions about the Kingdom of God, such as "When?" or "Where?" drew from him answers clothed in imagery, or what amounted to a flat "I don't know" (Mark 13:32). Whatever his thought processes may have been— and they were brilliant—they were carried out with natural endowments like ours. He had no special equipment, either physically or mentally; but what he had was good, and he used it well.

His approach to life was so different from ours that we have to look twice to see in it anything but destitution and drabness. Some of the out-of-step members of our modern civilization would have felt at home in it, however. "Simplify, simplify, simplify!" wrote Thoreau; and "A man is rich in proportion to the number of things which he can afford to let alone."

It all depends on how you look at it. From one point of view (the one which we habitually occupy) we are rich, happy, and comfortable among all our possessions; but from another we are like the ants we can see down among the grass blades, struggling along with burdens several times as large as they. It was a valid linguistic insight that led the Latin word for an army's heavy baggage to be derived from the verb *impedire,* to entangle or ensnare. That is what we surround ourselves with, all in the name of comfort and ease—*impedimenta.* How can anyone doubt it who has struggled to keep a lawn mowed, dust overstuffed furniture, balance a checkbook, or pay off a mortgage? Weighted down like this, how can we ever lift our heads to look around us at the world, and up into the sky?

From this point of view, Jesus begins to appear not *poor*, but *free.* This is certainly how he felt about it. "One thing you lack," he told a rich man. "Go, sell everything you have, and give to the poor, and you will have riches in heaven" (Mark 10:21). Like the rich man we may find this impossible to carry out literally; but to have possessions referred to as a "lack" is a new angle, to say the least, and we come away from the incident with a new insight into our harried "happiness."

Jesus was free. He carried no impediments on his life's journey. He owned no possessions, and so had no possessions to own him.

This attitude of his went far deeper than the most obvious application of it, to material possessions only. To understand it at all we must look at the extent to which we unconsciously make a possession of nearly everything that comes our way. We say "my family," "my plans," "my opinions," "my God"; and without our realizing it, this "my" comes to mean not responsibility and relationship, but ownership. Who does not know (possibly without looking outside his own skin) someone who makes a possession out of one or all of these relationships?

To Jesus, his family did not own him, nor he it; it was the environment that had nourished him. It had given him the basis of his insight into the relationship that is possible among human beings who acknowledge and carry out the purpose of the same Father, and from it he drew the image in which he described this relationship to his followers: "My mother and my brothers—they are those who hear the word of God and act upon it" (Luke 8:21).

His opinions, though strong and strongly held, were not his to clutch and keep; they belonged to the central truth in whose existence he believed and which, to him, it was the function of human thought to find and serve. On one occasion at least he is to be seen in the process of changing his mind (Mark 7:24–30); and he held that the refusal to recognize a fact or situation or truth that challenges a pet belief or prejudice is the one unforgivable act—a sin against the spirit of truth (Matthew 12:25–32).

His religion and his God, similarly, were in no sense possessions. Some of his sharpest remarks are directed at the people who use this area of their lives for outward displays of "nobility" or "goodness." Jesus seems to have felt that these people miss the whole point when they make property out of something that can exist only as a living relationship within the heart. "When you pray, go into a room by yourself, shut the door, and pray to your Father

who is there in the secret place; and your Father who sees
what is secret will reward you" (Matthew 6:6).

And what about plans? We think very favorably of a
man who has a plan for his life, for his family, the nation,
or the world. But plans have tyranny concealed in them:
they tend to take precedence over human values and sell
out the present in slavery to the future. They take hold
of the mind of a man or a nation—as we know when we
see a nation enslaved to its plan for a thousand-year Reich,
or a family never seeing its chief member because he has
a plan for their future and is away working on it day and
night. But if we are not to plan, what then? Where is any
unity or direction of life to be found?

Jesus seems to have been free from the tyranny of ordinary human plans. He evidently considered them futile,
at least in the areas in which we do most of our planning:
"Surely life is more than food, the body more than clothes"
(Matthew 6:25). And yet his life was clearly not aimless.
Its unity and continuity came, however, not from a pro-
gram or a plan, but from the day-by-day meeting of life in
the consistency of an attitude. He wandered around Judea,
meeting people, talking to them, working steadily along in
one unrelated situation after another. Without the usual
plans, he was free to meet each of these situations as it confronted him, freshly, creatively, out of the unity that was
within him.

So Jesus was free. But immediately the question comes
to mind, "Free for what?"

It is a good question, and Jesus both asks and answers
it himself, in a very interesting dialogue with the disciple
Peter. The question has come up whether or not to pay the
temple tax required of all devout Jews, and Jesus (who in
the end instructs Peter to pay the tax) uses the occasion for
a general comment about obligation. He asks Peter, "What

do you think, Simon? From whom do the kings of the earth take toll or tribute? From their sons, or from others?" Peter replies, "From others." And Jesus says, "Then the sons are free" (Matthew 17:25, 26, RSV).

In what way is a son free, if he is to be truly a son?

To find a good answer to this question we must approach it on two levels: first, what it means, always, to be a son; and second, what being a son meant to the Jews of Jesus' time.

A stock phrase, which everyone understands, may give us a clue to the first meaning: "He's his father's son all right," we say. This means to everyone who hears it that the boy is so much like his father that anyone can see their relationship. A son, always, has within him the freedom of his father's kind: he can move around in his father's world, using the environment his father gives him—physical, mental, spiritual—to grow toward being really at home in that world.

But the word "son" can mean even more than this, and in agricultural and pastoral societies like that of first-century Palestine, it still does. A son learns his father's occupation and is his right-hand man; he understands his father's purpose and makes carrying it out in obedience his own purpose and pleasure. "My boy, you are always with me, and everything I have is yours," the father says to his responsible, stay-at-home son in one of Jesus' most famous parables (Luke 15:30). This was the true sonship of that day—this close connection and interchange.

So there is an interesting twist to the idea of freedom, as Jesus presents it. We tend to think of freedom as freedom *from:* it means that we don't have to do something, aren't bound by anything. But to Jesus, freedom was freedom *to:* it meant being delivered from the blind obligation

of a slave or a subject, in order to serve freely in relationship and knowledge—and love.

   This, to Jesus, was freedom; this was sonship.

   "It happened at this time that Jesus came from Nazareth in Galilee and was baptized in the Jordan by John.
At the moment when he came up out of the water, he saw
the heavens torn open and the Spirit, like a dove, descend-
ing upon him. And a voice spoke from heaven: 'Thou art
my Son, my Beloved; on thee my favor rests'" (Mark 1:9–
11).

2

Jesus as Guide

"FOLLOW ME"—these are the words Jesus called out to four fishermen on the shore of the Sea of Galilee, men who became his first disciples. We think of the phrase as implying authority and unconsciously translate it as "Obey me." But what if Jesus means something else?

"Follow me." Perhaps these are not only the words of a ruler but also those of a guide, evoking a picture that goes back to the dawn of time and the depth of human experience. "I will show you the way," a man says, and people follow him through wild and unknown country, not sure where they are going, not sure how to get there, only sure that they have a guide whom they can trust.

One country remains perilous, however tamed-down the geographical ones may become—the wild unknown country of the self.

> O the mind, mind has mountains; cliffs of fall
> Frightful, sheer, no-man-fathomed. Hold them cheap
> May who ne'er hung there.*

More excruciatingly than in all previous centuries we are aware of this vast, bewildering interior, and of how easy it is to lose our way in it. We read, we talk, we search, we

* Gerard Manley Hopkins, *Poems* (London: Oxford University Press, 1953), p. 61. Used by permission.

go to psychiatrists, hoping to find a guide somewhere, somehow.

But do we ever look in the Gospels for Jesus' map of the self? And if we did, what would we find, and where would we find it?

At one point in the Matthew account, Jesus goes up on a mountain to teach the disciples—the men who thought he knew the way and had accepted him as guide. Twenty centuries have found guidance in these teachings, the famous Sermon on the Mount; perhaps we can too.

But if anything in the Gospels suffers from overfamiliarity, surely it is this Sermon. The words are worn as thin as old coins. People who know nothing else about Christianity can—and do, very often—quote the Golden Rule. Children are taught the Beatitudes so early and so thoroughly that they can parrot them the rest of their lives without a thought as to what they mean. Everybody knows that Jesus says, "Judge not." Everybody knows that he says, "Ask and it shall be given you." But as for what he means—well, it is like driving along a highway whose guiding signs have been out in the weather so long that they can no longer be read. How can we make them fresh and legible again?

One of the best ways is to begin with an objective look at the Sermon as a whole, to see what its themes and general outlines are—what it is, and (perhaps more important still) what it is not.

The Sermon appears most fully in Matthew—more briefly in Luke, with much variation between the two texts. Many passages in the Matthew Sermon are elsewhere in Luke, scattered through a portion of text that seems to be a miscellaneous collection of sayings. This last fact suggests that what Matthew presents as one discourse may actually be a compilation. A mental picture of someone with a pile of 3″ x 5″ cards in front of him, selecting and arranging according to topic, might not be totally out of keeping with the situation.

This compilation can be outlined as follows: a general descriptive introduction known to us as the Beatitudes; a long section, clear-cut and strongly patterned, on the Law; another section, also helpfully patterned, on ways of performing religious observances; a section on concern over material security; one on judgment; a series of short statements on various subjects; and a final summary topped off by the familiar parable of the two houses.

Seen in this way, the Sermon begins to look like rather a jumble. But this jumble has running through it one thread of continuity, a startling negative fact—the almost complete absence of any external or altruistic motive for action.

"How blest are those of a gentle spirit." Why? Because they give a good example to others? No—because "they shall have the earth for their possession" (Matthew 5:5).

"Do not store up for yourselves treasure on earth." Why not? Because the poor will go hungry, lacking what you keep? No—because "where your wealth is, there will your heart be also" (Matthew 6:19, 21).

"Pass no judgment." Why? Because you may be too hard on others? No—because "whatever measure you deal out to others will be dealt back to you" (Matthew 7:2).

The frame of reference could hardly be more individual. We look in vain for social concern, for some word about sharing with the poor, about the misuse of political, economic, or religious power, about good government or good relations among men. These concerns are to be found elsewhere in the teachings of Jesus, but not here. This Sermon is concerned with the individual; or to translate these words into others more startling, this Sermon tells us to be self-centered.

But this isn't what Christianity stands for! Jesus is against this! Doesn't he say, "Anyone who wishes to be a follower of mine must leave self behind" (Mark 8:34)?

Jesus' teaching about the self is not quite so simple as we might think. On the one hand he does say, "Leave self behind." But on the other he says, "Love your neighbor as yourself" (Matthew 22:39). *As yourself.* It looks as if altruism and social concern are to begin with and be guided by one's attitude toward oneself; and he calls this attitude "love."

What is love? Well, defining it can take a lifetime and more of living or writing or both, as Dante showed in his *Divine Comedy.* At the very least, loving is paying attention to, remembering, being concerned for—in short, not "leaving behind." Leaving oneself behind may come later in discipleship; but here, at the beginning, one pays attention to oneself. This is realistic; for anyone who looks into his heart knows that he can never "forget" himself by deciding to do so. Leaving oneself behind is a long process, a lifetime process, as long as learning to love—perhaps they are the same process? And it begins where Jesus begins it in this Sermon, with attention to oneself.

Let us see, then, how Jesus guides us through the country of the self—your self, my self, everyone's self. First comes the introductory passage of description, "How blest. . . ."

Right away we are in trouble, for this word "bless" is strictly a church-going word, without much meaning in everyday experience. The dictionary definition seems to point in two directions: first, "consecrated" or set apart; and second, "happy" or fortunate. "Happy" is the word used in several modern translations of the Gospels, just as *heureux* is the word used in French Bibles.

The self is to be happy or fortunate, then. But there follows a list of qualities that sound anything but fortunate. Some of them sound downright miserable, others so stripped-down and constrained as to be almost worse. They all seem to converge on a have-not state, while our everyday definitions of good fortune involve, almost without exception, *having*. Here are poverty, mourning, hunger, thirst, persecution. Blessed be leanness, in other words; happy are the thin. And here are mercy, meekness, purity, peacemaking—admirable qualities perhaps, but "fortunate"? That is not the word which we would spontaneously choose.

But Jesus chooses it; and he gives reasons. Hunger opens the way for being filled; poverty opens the way to riches; gentleness opens the whole wide earth. If we are full and content, that's that, the matter is closed; but if we are empty, there is room for the blessing to come in. Jesus is describing an open state, ready for the fullness of the Kingdom—for sonship and the service of God. He is describing the blessed self, not clutching and possessive, but open, expectant, ready to receive what comes to it. And is this so different from our own keenest observations and best experiences of happiness, good fortune, blessedness?

The general introduction continues: These happy selves have a task. They are consecrated, set apart in the world of human beings to be something that is as quiet and yet as all-pervasive as the action of salt or light in the physical world. They are "blessed" in both senses of the word.

The inner state of blessedness has been delineated now; its details are yet to be filled in. What, for instance, has it to do with Law, or Law with it? Is such an open, free self bound by Law? This important question was asked of

Jesus many times in his life. Here he answers it. "Do not suppose that I have come to abolish the Law and the prophets; I did not come to abolish, but to complete" (Matthew 5:17). The next section of the Sermon explains what he means.

Such a self as this lives not without, or this side of, the Law, but beyond and behind it, in the facts of human nature and human need out of which the laws spring. In his attitudes this self is to begin not with the law against murder, but with the inward states of anger, hatred, and contempt—from which the outward act of murder comes—which are as murderous to his own heart as the fires of hell, as chilling as a court of law. He is to concern himself not with the law against adultery, but with the fact that the man whom physical desire has mastered burns as if in hell and endures continually what Shakespeare describes as "the expense of spirit in a waste of shame." Similarly the law is, "Do not break your oath"; but behind that lies the fact that when a man needs an oath to validate his word, he has adopted a double standard of truth. A man must be all of one piece where truth is concerned: his Yes must be always Yes and his No always No—anything more complicated than this is "from the devil" (Matthew 5:33–37).

A kind of self is next described that seems almost impossible to imagine—one genuinely able to live by the directive "Do not set yourself against the man who wrongs you" (Matthew 5:39). What is not said here needs to be noticed as much as what is. What about the social evils of the world? What about harm that comes to other people? Are we supposed to stand by and let evil come about? Nothing is said here, one way or the other, about any of this; the area delineated is strictly the area of oneself. "If someone slaps you on the right cheek"—this is encroachment upon one's own physical being. "If a man wants to sue you for your shirt"—this is encroachment upon one's possessions. "If a man . . . makes you go one mile"—this is encroachment upon one's time and energy. And this we are supposed to take and like? Impossible! We might be able to force it on ourselves as a discipline, but to transmute it into a free gift, as Jesus seems to expect—this is beyond any self that we can find occupying our bodies at the present moment.

But is it? What about our lives with the people we love? Take our children, for instance: they can encroach on our time, energy, and possessions every day all day; sometimes if they are angry they may even strike us. Most of the time we struggle along swimming upstream against a strong current of resentment. But sometimes, on our best days, this continual gift of ourselves to them becomes a joy, not a task, and we can, while performing the exterior act that the situation demands (possibly even a spanking), interiorly turn the other cheek, give the coat, go the second mile. It is a moment of great freedom, when the little, resentful, self-protective "I" gives way to a larger unit of the self, a big "I," which acts, gives, and loves strongly enough to have no need of its usual boundaries.

This big "I" is what Jesus is pointing us toward; in the last portion of this section he delineates it more clearly. If we can extend the free attitude not only toward those we love, but toward those whom we have reason to hate, a great reward awaits us: complete deliverance from the small "I"—the ability to be "all goodness" toward people (Matthew 5:48), to be "children of your heavenly Father, who makes his sun rise on good and bad alike" (Matthew 5:45). It may or may not change the external situation— Jesus says nothing whatever about that—but this newfound

self is both the flower of a complete interior change and
its reward.

Reward—this is a theme that we are not much accus-
tomed to meeting in high-minded thinking. "Forget the
reward," we tell our children. "Don't be always thinking
what you're going to get out of it; do it for its own sake."
Jesus would disagree with us. He mentions a reward here,
and in the next section he develops the idea more fully.

Now the pattern-structure changes. "They have their
reward already. . . . Your Father . . . will reward you."
Three times this refrain is repeated and applied to acts that
are good in themselves—charitable giving, prayer, self-
denial (Matthew 6:2–18). But acts that are good in themselves may be very bad for us if we do them in the wrong
way, Jesus warns. "Be careful not to make a show of your
religion before men" (Matthew 6:1). This is the wrong
way because it brings a false reward, the approbation of
other men (and of oneself), and thus closes off completely
all chance of gaining the true reward. For the true reward
is not a result, but is hidden in the event itself, in the un-
divided attention that we give to the act and to the Father
who inspires it.

The next portion, like that on oath-taking, shows Jesus'
concern over division in this "secret place" of the self. "Do
not store up for yourselves treasure on earth. . . . Store
up treasure in heaven. . . . No servant can be slave to two
masters. . . . You cannot serve God and Money" (Matthew
6:19–24). This seems logical enough and gains at least our
intellectual assent; yet what follows seems fully as impossible to carry out as the earlier injunction to turn the other
cheek. Food, drink, clothes—surely they are necessary,
surely we need to take some thought for them? But Jesus
says, "All these are things for the heathen to run after, not

for you, because your heavenly Father knows that you need them all" (Matthew 6:32).

Again we need to turn inward to find the real point of Jesus' thought. Are we to give up working for food and clothing? No—the birds of whom he speaks hunt worms and build nests, the lilies in the fields send out roots and soak up sun in order to grow. We are to work, but we must "put away anxious thoughts," we must set our minds "on God's kingdom and his justice before everything else, and all the rest will come" (Matthew 6:25, 33). We must be so willing to be the mere human mortals that we are, so conscious that we are only parts of the whole, and so ready to live trustingly in the world that God has made, that what we have will come to us as our share of the Kingdom, not a broken piece of it (more than our share, probably) that we have snatched and clutched for ourselves. "Be not anxious" does not mean that trouble and deprivation will never come. It means that if we are living in the trusting way that Jesus describes, we shall be able to take it as it comes. "Tomorrow will look after itself. Each day has troubles enough of its own" (Matthew 6:34).

"What shall we live on?" is one large area of human anxiety; another, equally large, is "What will people think?" and this is what Jesus takes up next. As previously, he brings the matter back to the starting-place of the individual self. This judging business—clear it up in yourself first, and you will find the whole situation clearing up. "For as you judge others, so will you yourselves be judged" (Matthew 7:2). Our own judgmental attitudes come back on us in two ways. First, they set up an atmosphere around us that makes other people as harsh with us as they feel us to be with them. Second, and more centrally, the way we look at our world and the people in it is a most accurate measure of what is in our own hearts.

What we project, that we are; what we expect, that we are; what we look for, that we are. Envy, jealousy, cruelty, anger, hatred, treachery—we have found them (whether we know it or not) first in ourselves before we see them in others. What we are is the "plank" of the parable (Matthew 7:3–5) that blocks and distorts our vision. So "judge not" until you can see clearly; then you will want to help, not to judge. Then, too, you will be able to see the suitable action to take, the suitable time to act; you will no longer "feed your pearls to pigs" (Matthew 7:6).

There follows a short section on asking, reminiscent of the thought at the very beginning—Blessed are those who hunger—for "everyone who asks receives, he who seeks finds, and to him who knocks the door will be opened" (Matthew 7:8).

Then comes the sentence that everyone knows, the Golden Rule: "Always treat others as you would like them to treat you" (Matthew 7:12). "Love thy neighbor as thyself": it is the same equation, based upon the same foundation of unabashed self-reference that underlies this whole discourse.

But what is this that follows, about a narrow gate? It seems to come in oddly here, where we are hearing about the pleasant subject of our own likes and the way we want to be treated. Yet this is exactly where the narrow gate belongs. For the "wide gate" of self-reference is the one we would most readily think of here: what we like best, what is easiest or most comfortable for us, what gives us the most pleasure—the standards of the small "I." But the way to the larger "I" is through a much smaller gate than that, and along a much more constrained way. Jesus says, "Those who find it are few" (Matthew 7:14). Those who do not find it are "savage wolves" in all that they pretend to do for other people, however gentle and generous they may seem. As C. S. Lewis put it in his *Screwtape Letters:* "She's the sort of woman who lives for others—you can always tell the others by their hunted expressions."

No. Goodness and helpfulness toward others must grow out of the new self, not be put on as a covering over the old one. Jesus uses several gardening metaphors to point toward the organic unity of this process. "Can grapes be picked from briars, or figs from thistles? In the same way a good tree always yields good fruit and a poor tree bad fruit" (Matthew 7:17–18). Goodness is not a suit of clothes to put on; it is something that we grow into and that grows in us. Jesus has dealt with this idea in other ways—in the sayings about the single standard of truth (Matthew 5:33–37) and about the one-pointed simplicity of relationship with the Father (Matthew 6:1–6, 16–18).

This is all fine, but now what? How does one move toward the new self, the larger "I"? What is the bridge between hearing and being? Jesus' answer is *Do*. "Not everyone who calls me 'Lord, Lord' will enter the kingdom of Heaven, but only those who do the will of my heavenly Father" (Matthew 7:21). We are to act upon what we hear, in whatever infinitesimal way we can—but *act*. This is sound advice according to our own experience: We all know that we can listen to lectures on tennis all day, every day, but never can learn to play unless we go onto a court and begin hitting balls around. Then we build the muscles and acquire the skill that makes the game of tennis really ours and not merely an idea.

But what kind of action does this Sermon call for? Jesus has been healing and teaching (Matthew 4:23–25). Is that the kind of "doing" that he means? His answer is emphatic: "Many will say to me, 'Lord, Lord, did we not prophesy in your name, cast out devils in your name, and in your name perform many miracles?' Then I will tell them to their face, 'I never knew you; out of my sight, you and your wicked ways!' " (Matthew 7:22–23). No—the doing called for in this Sermon is not outward work (that comes later) but the inward work of acting upon what one understands about the self. It is not power over outward things but over the inner world where our desires live and grow. It is the interior discipline of our interior country.

If we do this, Jesus concludes, we build a house upon the rock, a self that will not break apart under the storms of life and death. We free ourselves from the tyrant who sits in the center of our hearts, craving, coveting, demanding. We gain the self that can live and love and serve, that can be an instrument in the work of God, that can see God and understand His mighty ways. This Sermon is the Good News of the new self,

> remade, reborn, like a sun-wakened tree
> that spreads new foliage to the Spring dew
> in sweetest freshness, healed of Winter's scars;
> perfect, pure, and ready for the stars.*

* Dante, *Purgatorio,* trans. John Ciardi (New York: New American Library, 1961), canto 33, ll. 143–146. Used by permission.

3

Jesus as Healer

SOME DAY IN THE HISTORY BOOKS our time may be called the Age of Healing. Never before has so much attention been paid to health or so much been done toward achieving it. One disease after another has been conquered; and we have almost come to feel that in this area nothing is impossible.

Because of our twentieth-century experiences with the power of healing, we might expect ourselves to be better prepared than any other period of history to understand and sympathize with the healings of Jesus as they are reported in the Gospels. And yet right at the outset something about them puts us off.

They are "miraculous"—sudden, unexplained events for which there is no scientific basis that we can see. All the laws of medicine as we know them seem to be contradicted —the patient research, the painstaking diagnosis, the slow process of healing. How could healing possibly come about in the way that the Gospels describe?

But we are giving the miracles entirely the wrong treatment if we ask first of all, "Did they really happen?"—a question characteristic of our modern age and scientific turn of thought. Jewish thought and the early Christian thought that produced the Gospels never asked it. The real question was for them—and still is for us—"What do they mean?"

The answer comes quickly from the texts. The miracles mean mercy, they mean compassion. In Matthew Jesus is shown quoting twice a word of God spoken by the prophet Hosea: "I desire mercy, and not sacrifice" (Matthew 9:13; 12:7, RSV). The Gospel of Luke gives a vivid picture of Jesus announcing to the people in his home town the meaning of his mission.

> He . . . went to synagogue on the Sabbath day as he regularly did. He stood up to read the lesson and was handed the scroll of the prophet Isaiah. He opened the scroll and found the passage which says,
> "The spirit of the Lord is upon me because he has
>   anointed me;
> He has sent me to announce good news to the poor,
> To proclaim release for prisoners and recovery of sight
>   for the blind;
> To let the broken victim go free,
> To proclaim the year of the Lord's favour."
> He rolled up the scroll, gave it back to the attendant, and sat down; and all eyes in the synagogue were fixed on him.
> (Luke 4:16-20)

The miracles mean mercy. This we, of the Age of Healing, can understand; and in this framework we can find ourselves at home in these events, rejoicing with the multitudes and praising God while people who have been paralyzed for years get up and walk at a word, blind men see, skin diseases fall away like old clothing, and men and women whose inner selves are shattered into fragments become functioning units once more. Could anything possibly be more wonderful, more important, more worth doing?

And yet what is the attitude of Jesus himself toward

these healings? Is he as pleased with them as we are? Does he consider them as important as we do?

The answer to these questions lies half-concealed in many episodes scattered through the Gospels; but we can find its beginning in the time of temptation in the desert that immediately follows Jesus' baptism. The Tempter says to him, "If you are the Son of God, tell this stone to become bread." But Jesus answers, "Scripture says, 'Man cannot live on bread alone'" (Luke 4:3-4). Here the Tempter assumes (and Jesus does not question) that to be Son of God means to have power—in this case power to feed himself and the multitudes, to end one of man's greatest miseries, hunger. Jesus' answer here might be adapted also to man's other greatest misery, illness: "Man's well-being does not lie in physical health alone."

In what then does it lie? The Old Testament passage from which Jesus quotes reads: "Man does not live by bread alone, but . . . man lives by everything that proceeds out of the mouth of the Lord" (Deuteronomy 8:3).

In the Temptations Jesus says No to material power, to political power, to the hypnotic power of dramatic action, and chooses instead the secret power that stirs up the inner world of the hearer—the quiet, inconspicuous work of teaching—to bring the word of God to men so that they may begin to live by it.

"Jesus came into Galilee proclaiming the Gospel of God: 'The time has come; the kingdom of God is upon you; repent and believe the Gospel'" (Mark 1:14-15).

And yet from the beginning of this quiet ministry, miracles and mighty works attend it—"powers," the Gospel of Luke calls them. An epileptic man cries out in a synagogue while Jesus is teaching. He is healed. Simon's mother-in-law has a high fever. She is healed. Word gets around and the whole city gathers together around the house. How can any real teaching take place in such a commotion as this?

"Very early next morning he got up and went out. He went away to a lonely spot and remained there in prayer. But Simon and his companions searched him out, found him, and said, 'They are all looking for you.' He answered, 'Let us move on to the country towns in the neighborhood; I have to proclaim my message there also; that is what I came out to do' " (Mark 1:35–38).

Thus affirmed, the teaching continues; but so also do the miracles; and Mark gives an interesting hint as to why and how. "Once he was approached by a leper, who knelt before him begging his help. 'If only you will,' said the man, 'you can cleanse me.' In warm indignation Jesus stretched out his hand, touched him, and said, 'Indeed I will; be clean again' " (Mark 1:40–41).

"In warm indignation"—or "moved with pity," as the Revised Standard Version puts it: here is not only "power subordinate to love," as William Temple says, but power drawn forth by love, tapped by human need as electricity is tapped by plugging into an outlet in a wall.

Jesus tries to keep the results of this flowing-forth under control; he tells the man not to spread any word of it. "But the man went out and made the whole story public; he spread it far and wide, until Jesus could no longer show himself in any town, but stayed outside in the open country. Even so, people kept coming to him from all quarters" (Mark 1:45).

What is to be done? Is the teaching to be lost in the crush of the crowds, submerged under this surging demand for healing?

The next episode, which follows (according to Luke) a time of prayer, shows an impressive leap of thought. Jesus comes back to the town, a crowd gathers, and he is teaching a group inside a house when there is a commotion: a section of the roof is torn off, and a paralyzed man is let down on ropes through the hole. The teaching stops—but does it stop? or only change? Jesus does not at first heal the man; he says to him, "My son, your sins are forgiven." This inward healing, not that of the body, is the important one. Only after his statement has been questioned does Jesus affirm it and his right to say it by healing the body as well as the soul (Mark 2:1–12).

Here is a fusion of elements previously in tension: the teaching is part of the healing, the healing is part of the teaching. So it continues throughout the Gospels: healings take place, but they never again threaten the main work.

In fact, they support it, because they open the way for one of Jesus' most important and all-pervading subjects of thought, teaching, and example—faith. In almost every healing episode Jesus points to something within the seeking person himself as the source of healing; and he always calls it by the same name—faith.

One of the stories illustrates this dramatically. Jesus and the disciples are in a densely packed crowd, and suddenly Jesus says, "Who was it that touched me?" Peter and the others are understandably bewildered. "Master, the crowds are hemming you in and pressing upon you!" they say. But Jesus still persists: "Someone did touch me, for I felt that power had gone out from me." But when a woman confesses that she has secretly touched his robe in a desire to be healed, he attributes the healing not to what has gone forth from him, but to something in her. "My daughter, your faith has cured you. Go in peace" (Luke 8:43–48).

"Faith" is an enormous word, so large that it tends to have no meaning at all; and other large words that we might substitute for it—"belief," "trust," "confidence"—do not help us much. Perhaps the best way to come at what

Jesus meant by it is to treat it as if it were a totally unknown word, whose meaning we are trying to establish by the various contexts in which we find it.

Of the men who tore the hole in the roof for their friend it is said that Jesus "saw their faith." What did he see that we too can see in the story? Damaging a roof and breaking rudely into a serious and important occasion might get a lot of words out of us, but hardly that one.

Then, too, there is a woman, conscious not of sickness but of sin, who comes into a dignified dinner party and makes what, to our eyes, is a scene over Jesus. "His feet were wetted with her tears and she wiped them with her hair, kissing them and anointing them with the myrrh." Jesus says to her what he said to the woman who forced her way through the crowd to touch him: "Your faith has saved you; go in peace" (Luke 7:36–50).

In these episodes Jesus seems to see need, emptiness, hope—and a drive to satisfy them that is too strong for any merely prudential or social considerations to block. He sees *asking* in its purest form, as simple and direct as hunger. "How blest are you who now go hungry; your hunger shall be satisfied" (Luke 6:21).

This asking faith has the drive of the whole person behind it; and the Gospels show how it is expressed through two very different people—the weeping woman we have seen above, and a Roman captain who wanted his sick slave healed (Luke 7:1–10). The woman comes in a surge of emotion; and this is called "faith." The centurion's approach is a thoughtful, imaginative one; and this too is called "faith." The pattern of faith, evidently, can be as large as the number of individuals who hunger and seek and find.

Faith springs, furthermore, not only out of one's character and disposition, but out of one's experience as well.

The thoughtful centurion has evidently been asking himself some questions about this Source of Power that he is approaching; and he finds the answer—an answer that delights Jesus—through an analogy with his own experience. He himself has power within the Roman military hierarchy: "In my position I am myself under orders, with soldiers under me." He knows that he has power only because he is the transmitter of the Roman emperor's power; and extrapolating from this, he knows that Jesus has power because he is the transmitter of God's power. And Jesus calls this "faith" (Luke 7:8–9). Faith begins with experience, and moves from the known to the unknown by rightly understanding and feeling that experience.

Any honest impulse, any direct bringing of the whole person to Jesus, will do for a beginning. But Jesus expects faith to grow. "If you have faith no bigger even than a mustard-seed . . ." he says to the disciples once (Matthew 17:20); and in another place he tells a parable: "As a seed, mustard is smaller than any other; but when it has grown it is bigger than any garden-plant; it becomes a tree, big enough for the birds to come and roost among its branches" (Matthew 13:31–32).

As part of this growth process, Jesus seems to expect faith to free itself of externals and material aids and find its own interior strength. He seems to expect faith to free itself from fear—fear of failure, disaster, even death. In one of the Gospel stories, the disciples are terrified by a sudden storm on the lake (Jesus himself is asleep in the stern of the boat), and he says when they wake him, "Why are you such cowards? Have you no faith even now?" Their turning to him for help is not called faith, as it might have been earlier; apparently he thinks that by now they should be able to handle their own need-seek-find cycle of faith without him as intermediary (Mark 4:37–40).

The disciples themselves are puzzled by their inability to have faith. In another story, they fail in an attempt to heal an epileptic boy and come to Jesus afterwards to ask what holds them back from tapping this power which comes, apparently so easily, to him (Matthew 17:19-20).

Apparently so easily—is this really so? Or can we see, in what the Gospels report Jesus as saying and doing, signs of limits and laws for this world of faith in which he lives?

The time in the desert, immediately after the Baptism, has established many of these limits. Satan demands proof of Jesus' power; but Jesus knows that faith must not be used to convince himself or anyone else of its power. He does not use the power of God for his own physical satisfactions or needs, for his own personal aggrandizement, or to impress people. He does not test God by putting himself into perilous situations and then challenging God to produce a saving miracle. In everyday living, this means prudence—not the stuffy, self-saving quality that we have made this word represent, but a technique of doing dangerous and unusual things in the safest and most down-to-earth way possible. If we look at the Gospels with this in mind, we can see that, though Jesus does many dangerous and (from some points of view) "foolish" things, he never goes about them either dangerously or foolishly.

Later on other limits are established. A story in Matthew indicates a need for self-forgetfulness in faith: Peter sees Jesus walking on the water and wants to walk on it too; but when he is halfway from the boat to Jesus, the enormity of it all comes over him, and he begins to sink. "Jesus at once reached out and caught hold of him, and said, 'Why did you hesitate? How little faith you have!' " (Matthew 14:31). Here hesitation ("doubt" in other translations) is almost equated with self-consciousness, the kind of thing that gets in the way when one begins to stop and think while making a tennis shot or executing a skiing turn.

Faith demands that one cut loose from all the security of this world. "A doctor of the law came up and said, 'Master, I will follow you wherever you go.' Jesus replied, 'Foxes have their holes, the birds their roosts; but the Son of Man has nowhere to lay his head' " (Matthew 8:19–20).

The world of faith begins to look bare and stripped down. It is no wonder that Jesus speaks of a narrow gate, and once exclaims, "How hampered I am!" The promises of faith are tremendous, but they can be carried out only within this framework of self-consistency and self-limitation—the kind of limitation that we mean when we say of an honest man, "Oh, he couldn't possibly steal!" The operation of faith is limited not by exterior possibility, but by the consistency of its own nature. Jesus' largest promise shows this: "Have faith in God. I tell you this: if anyone says to this mountain, 'Be lifted from your place and hurled into the sea,' and has no inward doubts, but believes that what he says is happening, it will be done for him. I tell you, then, whatever you ask for in prayer, believe that you have received it and it will be yours" (Mark 11:22–25).

"Have faith *in God.*" If faith is *in God,* it will be guided by what we are able to know and understand of His nature. Faith is not a making real of the phrase, "I can dream, can't I?" but a relationship with the largest reality, God.

"And has no inward doubts." Faith must also be in genuine relationship to the reality we are most aware of, ourselves. We cannot bring only the firm will, determined to accomplish something, to faith: we must bring our whole selves and base our faith so securely on what we are and know by our own experience that we do not have doubts.

"Whatever you ask for *in prayer.*" The two relationships, to ourselves and to God, must be brought together in prayer. Prayer is a strange process. We begin by asking something of it; but it turns and asks something of us, and in the end, both we and what we ask are changed; and so we grow, and so does our prayer. It is within this context of prayer that all things are possible to faith.

We can see this process at work in Jesus himself, in the Garden of Gethsemane, just before his arrest. "He went forward a little, threw himself on the ground, and prayed that, if it were possible, this hour might pass him by. 'Abba, Father,' he said, 'all things are possible to thee; take this cup away from me. Yet not what I will, but what thou wilt' " (Mark 14:35–36). Jesus is aware of the reality within him—his horror of what is ahead—and he asks that the future may be changed. But his faith is in God, not in his wish; and so the prayer becomes a process within him, and ends on a larger note than the one on which it began.

Now he comes to the moment on the Cross that is the purest expression of faith: the stripped-down moment when all external helps have failed and even the inward light seems quenched, "the hour when darkness reigns" (Luke 22:53), and God is nowhere to be seen or felt. Yet Jesus can still call to Him, still reach out into the emptiness, still say, "My God," and ask why he has been forsaken—and die.

To this moment of pure faith, lived nearly two thousand years ago, all things were possible. It ended the irreversible finality of death; it healed the hearts and souls of the men who were left behind and sent them out to change history. What had begun with the healing of bodies had become far more. Of the Cross it can be truly said, "The leaves of the tree were for the healing of the nations" (Revelation 22:2, RSV).

4

Jesus as Teacher

THE FACT THAT Jesus chose teaching for his lifework
should impress us more than it does. In our culture teaching has acquired itself a pigeonhole as one of the profes-
sions, ranking in the general esteem well below law and
medicine. But what is teaching really, if we stop to look?
Parental as well as professional, private as well as public,
it is an activity that all of us take part in and that goes on
all the time.

It is the activity that makes us human.

For what would happen if all teaching were to stop tomorrow? In one generation, no more, everything we have
would be lost. Our grandchildren would look with blank
eyes and foggy minds at houses, machinery, tools, books.
They would have no skills, no words, no store of facts from
which to draw ideas and concepts. They would know that
they were hungry or sleepy, that they felt desire or fear or
anger; and that would be all.

Biological continuity can transmit only animal life. It
is teaching that opens up the rich possibilities of human
life. And it is teaching that can open up the possibility of
greater richness still. Jesus came, the Gospel of John tells
us, in order that people "may have life, and may have it
in all its fullness" (John 10:10). To accomplish his objec-

tive he chose to be a teacher; what else could he possibly
have chosen?

"When he came ashore, he saw a great crowd; and
his heart went out to them, because they were like sheep
without a shepherd; and he had much to teach them"
(Mark 6:34). This passage introduces an episode which
at first glance seems completely unrelated to it—the miracle by which thousands of people were fed with food
touched and divided by Jesus, a very small amount somehow becoming enough to feed them all. And yet is it so
unrelated? Perhaps, among other things, it is a living parable about teaching—that one man can feed many, and that
there is enough for all.

Where did Jesus learn what he taught? The Gospels are
largely silent on this point. One picture shows a boy spell-
bound by the studies going on in the Temple (Luke 2:46–
47). Another indicates that he had felt the impact of John
the Baptist's message, "Repent, for the kingdom of Heaven
is upon you" (Matthew 4:17). There are other hints: the
strong implication from his frequent and effective use of
quotations that he had learned the Old Testament almost
by heart; the suggestion from his use of anecdote and example that he had observed the world around him; the
impression given by his keen and sensitive approach to
law and custom that he had been well grounded in his
tradition.

What he learned he made his own. "The people were
astounded at his teaching, for, unlike the doctors of the
law, he taught with a note of authority" (Mark 1:22). The
doctors of the law, or scribes, taught strictly out of the
book, interpreting point by point. What Jesus taught was
grounded in Jewish tradition and often derived as closely
from the Old Testament as anything the scribes had to say;
yet it seemed to come not from the book, but out of his

own center and power. We have all known teachers who breathe their own life into what they teach; Jesus epitomized this quality.

Some teachers can challenge, but fail at encouraging. Some can teach a group but have nothing to give an individual; others work well privately but fail in public. Some can work in a favorable atmosphere but wilt in a chilly one. Jesus taught wherever he was—with one person, in a crowd, among friends, enemies, casual listeners, good churchmen, slick politicians, quislings, collaborationists, drunks, and prostitutes—and though he varied his method, his aim was always the same.

What was he trying to teach? The most difficult thing on earth—the Will of God, the Way of God, or, as he most often called it, the Kingdom of God. Once he said to Peter in rebuke, "You are a hindrance to me; for you are not on the side of God, but of men" (Matthew 16:23, RSV). He wanted to show men how to be on God's side, how to keep from hindering the gracious free power of God in themselves and in the world: how to allow (and help) the Kingdom of God to come.

The people to whom he brought this message fell into three major groups: the rigid traditionalists, doctors of the law and Pharisees, who felt themselves to be at the center of the Jewish religion; the formless crowd, made up of all kinds of people, Jew and Gentile; and the people who came out of the crowd to be his disciples. With each group he pursued a different teaching method—not by accident, but out of deliberate choice, clearly, for the pattern of approach seldom varies.

This pattern is outlined distinctly in Mark 7:1–23. The traditionalists come to challenge Jesus on a point of order. He deals with them in a logical, systematic way, countering their reference to tradition with two of his own, one from the law and one from the prophets. Then he turns to the crowd and gives them a short, cryptic parable, a signpost merely, pointing toward the deeper meaning of what he has said to the scribes and Pharisees. Later still, alone with the disciples, he fully explains his thought.

A challenge and an argument for those whose minds are fixed; a hint for those who are neither here nor there; with explanation reserved for those who are eager to learn. Why?

In dealing with the scribes and Pharisees, Jesus is trying a very difficult piece of work—the job of making people who think they know all about something look into it afresh for a deep insight that they have lost or never known. With this group he is meeting deadly opposition, and he knows it; but even here he is ready to teach. They see him as a law-breaker and destroyer of tradition. He would like to show them otherwise: "Do not suppose that I have come to abolish the Law and the prophets; I did not come to abolish, but to complete" (Matthew 5:17). Yes, but how can he convince them of this? He uses their own line of thought, their own method of inquiry, the use of logic and the searching of Scripture, in an attempt to show them a different world and a different God from the one they have found.

Again and again with this group we can see the same technique at work—the appeal to the book, to tradition, or to experience to show them something deeper than they have yet seen. "Have you never read what David did?" (Mark 2:25). "Is it permitted to do good or to do evil on the Sabbath?" (Mark 3:4). "How can Satan drive out Satan?" (Mark 3:23). Even in the sharpest sayings of all, the series beginning, "Alas for you, lawyers and Pharisees . . ." (Matthew 23:13–36), Jesus is still teaching, still trying to show the traditionalists the perils of their kind of rigid "righteousness."

But the task is backbreaking; and though Jesus never gives up, he comes, like John the Baptist, to feel that the hardened heart of a tradition is its least redeemable part. "Many, I tell you, will come from east and west to feast with Abraham, Isaac, and Jacob in the kingdom of Heaven. But those who were born to the kingdom will be driven out into the dark" (Matthew 8:11–12). Here, as so often in Jesus' teaching, the future tense represents more the statement of a present inner condition than the threat of a future external one.

The crowds are different, neither hostile nor friendly, simply listening—who can tell what will come out of them? —and with them his technique is quite different. He uses not reasoning nor the logical appeal to tradition, but a story, brief, vivid, memorable. He tells such a story and then calls out, "If you have ears to hear, then hear" (Luke 8:8).

The disciples, puzzled by this, come to him and ask what the parable means.

Jesus reassures them, and goes on to make a statement that has startled many a generation. As so often, he quotes Isaiah (which must rank second only to the Psalms as a favorite book of his). He speaks in parables to others, he says, "in order that they may look but see nothing, hear but understand nothing" (Luke 8:10; Isaiah 6:3). Here is a teaching method carefully designed, apparently, *not* to teach. Why? What kind of teaching is this?

Actually it is the essential beginning of good teaching. Who cannot remember, somewhere in his own schooling, a teacher who asked questions, who suggested a mystery, who so roused curiosity that it had to be satisfied? Who cannot remember how the learning process flew on its own wings, started off like this?

A parable is the perfect tool for such a beginning. It has the indirect, one-pointed quality of a joke, and like a joke is complete in itself, implying rather than stating the real purpose for which it was told. It does not tell outright: it hints, suggests, puzzles, challenges. Sometimes defined as "an earthly story with a heavenly meaning," it teaches unfamiliar things in terms of the familiar, bridging the gap between known and unknown. By its deceptive simplicity it relaxes people into seeing something that in ordinary wariness they would refuse to look at—as Lincoln knew when he used jokes to make sensitive points with members of his cabinet and staff.

A parable is not open to logical understanding, any more than a joke yields its meaning to a mathematical analysis. It goes straight from one intuitive center to another and is by nature impervious to the impervious. You don't get it? Well, then, you don't get it, and it is impossible for you to fool yourself into thinking that you do. A parable is not likely to show anything but its smiling childlike surface to a fixed or stuffy mind, or to one occupying another world of reference.

But where it meets the response at which it was aimed, it flashes across, instantaneous and illuminating as lightning. To illustrate this quality, Jesus tells a parable describing the different kinds of ground which receive the seed, only one of which brings forth grain "a hundredfold." And he adds, "Take care, then, how you listen; for the man who has will be given more, and the man who has not will forfeit even what he thinks he has" (Luke 8:18). Listening is at least half of the teaching process; and the good teacher is one who from the beginning puts this part of the responsibility where it belongs. If the student will take in what he hears, more and more will be comprehensible to him; but if he loafs or resists, knowledge will quickly pass him by, and he will lose his grip on the little he has.

The parable method of teaching is a good selecting device as well; like an IBM machine it picks out of a large, assorted batch just the ones needed for a particular purpose. Or to take an image closer to Jesus' time—and very close to his own thought—a parable is like a baited hook. It is a fisher of men, and draws those to whom a certain way of life and thought appeals. So Jesus tells his parables to the crowd. Everybody listens. Some raise their eyebrows and turn away in scorn; it is too naïve for them, a child could think like that. Others are baffled, they just don't get it. But some respond. This teaching touches off something in them, and they come forward out of the crowd to meet the teacher face to face.

These are the disciples, the twelve of the inmost group and the larger, less well-defined band of followers who accompany Jesus on his journey to Jerusalem and to death.

Is this to be an in-group, sharply separated from the rest of the world, living in the center of a mystery and learning secrets carefully kept from outsiders? During the questioning about parables mentioned earlier, Jesus says something that might seem to bear out this idea. "To you," he tells the disciples, "the secret of the kingdom of God has been given; but to those who are outside everything comes by way of parables" (Mark 4:11). And the narrator sums up: "With many such parables he would give them his message, so far as they were able to receive it. He never spoke to them except in parables; but privately to his disciples he explained everything" (Mark 4:33–34).

Is this exclusiveness? The answer lies in the phrase "so far as they were able to receive it." The group of disciples

is exactly as exclusive, and in exactly the same way and for
the same reasons, as a seminar in advanced physics is exclusive. Its door is wide open to anyone who is able to understand what is being taught; but few are willing or feel
called to put themselves in the position of acquiring that
ability. So with Jesus' teaching: Anyone who chooses to
put himself in the right state for learning will be chosen;
but few choose to take the necessary steps.

However far the teaching of such a group may go, it
begins at exactly the point where casual attention turns
into deep interest. There is no break in the line of Jesus'
teaching between what he says to the crowd and what he
says to the disciples—no change of subject, only a change
of method. "You do not understand this parable?" he asks
the disciples. "How then are you to understand any parable?" (Mark 4:13). And he begins to explain.

With an eager group it is sound technique to expound,
lecture, explain; they will soak it up like thirsty ground.
Such teaching as that in the Sermon on the Mount (addressed, the Gospels of both Matthew and Luke tell us, directly to the disciples) may represent memories of this
direct, untrammeled passing on of knowledge and insight
to minds and hearts that are ready for it.

But the receiving of knowledge is by no means all there
is to learning. Basic human attitudes of intellectual rigidity (like that of the traditionalists) and of personal aim-
lessness (like that of the crowd) are not shed the instant a
man becomes a disciple; and Jesus' dealings with his inner
group show awareness of this fact. Granted that a man is
willing and eager, how is he to learn through and through;
how is he to be genuinely changed, made into a new man
who will be effective in his chosen field? This is the most
important work to be done in the making of a disciple of

the Kingdom of God, just as in the making of an astronaut or a scientist.

Jesus chose twelve out of this larger group; and with them we can see his work at its most concentrated. Twelve or thereabouts is a good size for a group—large enough for variety in types of personality and points of view to show itself, but small enough for each person to be freely and fully himself; small enough for each member to have a personal relationship with the teacher, but large enough to keep this relationship from becoming ingrown and over-intense.

Training begins, continues, and ends with being in the company of a person who is doing something well—with doing what you see done and becoming what you see. Mark puts this in a deceptively simple phrase: "He appointed twelve, to be with him" (Mark 3:14*a*, RSV). With him they can become more and more able to see, as awareness grows, how he operates in each situation and what each situation means to him. How he handles people, what he says, what he does—all these things will show them, day by day, what his values are and how he goes about putting them into practice.

A second step follows on this. They are to do what they see done, to learn (by setting themselves inside the same situation) what goes on inside the teacher as he does these things. They are "to be sent out to preach and have authority to cast out demons" (Mark 3:14*b*–15, RSV).

They begin, and often (how could it be otherwise?) they fail. Jesus meets these failures with the controlled mixture of patience and impatience that is characteristic of all deeply concerned teaching. They lose their nerve in a dangerous lake crossing, and he says, "Where is your faith?" (Luke 8:25). They fail to heal an epileptic boy and are told that their habits of prayer must grow. They want

to destroy a town whose inhabitants have been rude to
Jesus, and he says, "You do not know to what spirit you
belong" (Luke 9:55, note). They want to keep children
from bothering him, and he tells them that children have
a quality that all seekers after the Kingdom need. They
dispute over status, and he says that greatness is not what
people think it is. "The highest among you must bear
himself like the youngest, the chief of you like a servant.
. . . Here am I among you like a servant" (Luke 22:26–27).

An attitude is being delineated for each member of the
group. Slowly put together, tiny point by point, an inner
area is being marked out for them to occupy; and sometimes they get clear views of it. But then the clouds gather,
or they descend from their high place and lose the vision.
None of it is theirs yet. The teacher must do one more
thing to make his gift of insight and knowledge complete.

He must go away. He must leave them alone with what
they have learned, so that they will find it within themselves and not have to turn to him for it. A passage in the
Gospel of John makes eternal poetry of this everyday fact.
"I will ask the Father, and he will give you another to be
your Advocate, who will be with you for ever—the Spirit
of truth. . . . Your Advocate, the Holy Spirit . . . will teach
you everything, and will call to mind all that I have told
you. . . . It is for your good that I am leaving you. If I
do not go, your Advocate will not come" (John 14:16, 26;
16:7).

When he goes, they will seem to themselves to lose
everything; they will fall and fail and desert what they
have learned. But that too is part of the process, for they
will come back, made firm by failure and repentance; and
then, when they have taught themselves to wait and hope,
what they have learned will be genuinely theirs.

And so He goes, as it is written of Him; and comes **tri-**

umphant, when they least expect it, to bring them the final synthesis of what He has taught. "Then he opened their minds to understand the scriptures, and said . . . 'Behold, I send the promise of my Father upon you; but stay in the city, until you are clothed with power from on high' " (Luke 24:45–46, 49, RSV). And He sent them forth, having been remade, to remake the world.

5

Jesus as Humorist

As GREAT MEN step back into history, where does their humor go? The Cheshire Cat in *Alice in Wonderland* faded away slowly, its grin vanishing last. It is the reverse with our heroes—the smile vanishes first.

Lincoln as a humanitarian and statesman is famous throughout the world, but relatively few people know him as the great humorist and irrepressible clown that he was. Yet Lincoln died only a hundred years ago, and his jokes were remembered and written down.

Was Socrates humorous? In Plato's *Dialogues* one can sometimes hear, as if over a great distance, the faint echo of a laugh, enough to make one long to hear the full sound of it.

And Jesus—what about him? Had he any humor? Did he ever laugh? Did he ever make other people laugh?

It is almost impossible to tell. We are inhibited. He has been worshiped for twenty centuries; time and awe have done their work on him.

The solemnizing process is already at work in the Gospels themselves, as we can see in an incident reported in Matthew and Mark—Mark being generally accepted as the earlier of the two and a source for Matthew here, as throughout. In both versions a woman with a mentally disturbed daughter comes to ask help of Jesus. The Marcan account continues:

> She begged him to drive the spirit out of her daughter. He said to her, "Let the children be satisfied first; it is not fair to take the children's bread and throw it to the dogs." "Sir," she answered, "even the dogs under the table eat the children's scraps." He said to her, "For saying that, you may go home content; the unclean spirit has gone out of your daughter." (Mark 7:26–29)

Must we be deaf to the tone of this dialogue just because it is in Scripture? Jesus sums up the whole heavy subject of Jewish exclusiveness in a light and graceful image of children at their supper. The woman, fielding the figure of speech, returns it cleverly adapted to her need. It is an exchange of wit, sparkling and allusive, a dance of dialogue. And Jesus seems to enjoy it—to savor her unquenchability and the witty way it is expressed. Maybe he even smiled at her, who knows? Maybe they smiled at each other.

But now here is Matthew's account:

> The woman came and fell at his feet and cried, "Help me, sir." To this Jesus replied, "It is not right to take the children's bread and throw it to the dogs." "True, sir," she answered; "and yet the dogs eat the scraps that fall from their masters' table." Hearing this Jesus replied, "Woman, what faith you have! Be it as you wish!" (Matthew 15:25–28)

The changes are slight, but they alter the tone completely. "Fell at his feet—it is not right—masters' table—what faith." Worship and awe have replaced repartee; solemnity has set in.

And the trend has continued. What can we do to reverse it?

We can lighten our hearts and minds. We can stop taking the Gospels absolutely straight—stop making arithmetic

lessons ($2+2=4$) out of the teachings they contain. As
we listen to Jesus talking, we can keep our ears tuned for
such humorist's skills as exaggeration, wild images and
comparisons, satire and irony—the whole apparatus of wit,
the technique of the light touch. And maybe—who knows?
—we shall find the lost smile on the face of Jesus, especially
if we are willing to work with hints and glancing sugges-
tions, distant echoes, the faint traces that may remain after
solemnity has done its work.

To begin with, then, what indications are there in the
Gospels that Jesus ever laughed at life? Did he, like
Chaucer and Mark Twain, observe and enjoy the quirks
and inconsistencies of human nature, the whole happy
spectacle of humanity doing all the entertaining things
that come naturally to it?

There are many characters, closely observed and sharply
etched, going about their business in the stories Jesus tells.
A man finds his way like a homing pigeon to the top-
ranking seat at a banquet (Luke 14:7–8). A woman turns
her house upside down to find something she has lost
(Luke 15:8). Children complain because their friends
won't play the game they want (Matthew 11:16–17). A
young man sulks over the present his father has given to
his younger brother (Luke 15:28–30). A lazy son makes
promises to his father that he has no intention of keeping
(Matthew 21:29). A man nods his head approvingly over
a cup of old wine (Luke 5:39). Guests make last-minute
excuses to get out of a dinner invitation (Luke 14:18–20).

People with religious pretensions come under especially
sharp observation. Here is one thanking God that, unlike
some others he could mention, he is a good man (Luke
18:11–12). Here is one having a trumpet blown when he
makes a donation to charity; another praying with deep
and conspicuous concentration on a street corner; another

wearing a long, hungry face during a fast (Matthew 6:2, 5, 16). And here is a whole crowd strutting in long robes with wide borders, walking where everyone will be sure to notice them and be impressed (Matthew 23:5–7).

A kind of close and cheerful knowledge goes into the nicknames Jesus gives his disciples. James and John, who once want to call down fire on a village which has refused to welcome them (Luke 9:54), he calls "Sons of Thunder" (Mark 3:17). And there is a distinct possibility of irony in the nickname of Peter, or "Rock," given to Simon, who appears throughout the Gospels as quick to speak, often without thinking, quick to act, quick to swing from one extreme to another.

Camels are funny animals—all you have to do is look, and you're laughing. Jesus makes use of them in ways that call for drawings by Dr. Seuss. One camel is being swallowed by the religious characters already seen and described, as a vivid illustration of misplaced tolerance (Matthew 23:24); and another is trying to get through the eye of a needle, hump and all, in a thumbnail sketch of how hard it is for rich people to get into heaven (Mark 10:25). There is that ridiculous plank, too, in the eye of the man who is being critical of a speck of sawdust in someone else's eye (Matthew 7:3). It is easy to imagine both Jesus and the crowd laughing when that bit of exaggeration comes out—unless of course we assume (as we seem to) that first-century Palestinians never laughed.

Jesus seems to take joy in piling up images—so much so that one can imagine a listener who savors this kind of thing asking himself in fascinated wonder what on earth is coming next. The Kingdom of God, for example, is compared in turn to a farmer and his hired hands arguing about when to weed the south forty (Matthew 13:27–30); to a stalk of wheat (Mark 4:26–29); to a tall weedy plant with birds nesting in it, to yeast mixed into a batch of dough, to a buried treasure, to one pearl, to a dragnet full of fish (Matthew 13:31-33, 44-48). And the kind of wakefulness and awareness needed to make one ready for its coming are like many things: being a doorman (Mark 13:34); sitting up all night to catch a thief, working even when the boss isn't watching, getting ready for a wedding, investing money, feeding a hungry stranger (Matthew 24:42-25:40). The images blaze out as if from a Roman candle, with one more still to come when you think the show is over—it is an astonishing display. "And the great throng heard him gladly" (Mark 12:37, RSV). No wonder.

Well—humor is fun, and verbal fireworks put on a good show, but where does the serious teaching come in? Where is the religion?

A story from outside our own religious tradition may help to answer that question.

> Tanzan and Ekido were once travelling together down a muddy road. A heavy rain was still falling.
>
> Coming round a bend, they met a lovely girl in a silk kimono and sash, unable to cross at the intersection.
>
> "Come on, girl," said Tanzan at once. Lifting her in his arms, he carried her over the mud.
>
> Ekido did not speak again until that night when they reached a lodging temple. Then he could no longer restrain himself. "We monks don't go near females," he told Tanzan. "Especially not young and lovely ones. It is dangerous. Why did you do that?"
>
> "I left the girl there," said Tanzan. "Are you still carrying her?" *

This is a serious story, dealing with the basic problem of a religious person's relation to worldly temptations; yet it makes us laugh. It is a joke. There is no 2+2=4 about

---

* Paul Reps, ed., "101 Zen Stories," from *Zen Flesh, Zen Bones* (Rutland, Vt.: Charles E. Tuttle, 1957), p. 33. Used by permission.

it; it goes along with deceptive quietness, exploding all at once in one's face at the end. Humor and seriousness combine to make one organic whole; and the point of the story comes clear not out there on the page of the text, but within the reader at his moment of insight—a point that could never be made so well by a flat statement such as, for example, "The danger of outside things lies in their power over your mind." And in fact that may not be the single point of the story; it may say many different things to different readers. For that is the beauty of a joke—it does not pin things down. When it presents a truth, that truth has a life of its own and can speak to different hearts in different ways.

All of this raises the question whether we 2+2's have not robbed the teaching of Jesus of half its power by refusing to let it work within us with the free and creative seriousness of the joke.

Take prayer, for instance—surely a serious subject. Jesus tells two stories to illustrate the need for constant prayer; but they are not serious stories.

A man comes clamoring at your door in the middle of the night. You shout out the window, "Do not bother me. The door is shut for the night; my children and I have gone to bed; and I cannot get up and give you what you want" (Luke 11:5–8). But he keeps right on banging and shouting; so in the end you get up—not out of kindness, but simply to get rid of the noise—and give him what he wants.

Or you are a corrupt judge, and there is a woman who keeps after you to right an injustice for her. "True, I care nothing for God or man," you say to yourself; "but this widow is so great a nuisance that I will see her righted before she wears me out with her persistence" (Luke 18:2–5).

We shake our heads. Old $2+2=4$ is still with us. "God is neither fair nor just if he answers prayer for the same reason as the judge or the man in bed," we say carefully. But that's not the point! That's not what we are supposed to look at. Something is operating in these stories that cannot be taken at face value. These images, by their very inappropriateness, say something that images as good but more respectable could never say. They jolt you, they jar you; they make it impossible for you to take them quite straight. They demand that you let them live in your mind and work there, while you chew on them like a dog at a bone.

A prime example is the story of the shifty steward who, when he knew that he was going to be fired, settled his master's accounts privately for fifty cents on the dollar in order to make friends who would help him when he lost his job. Fine goings-on. But Jesus concludes soberly (it sounds somehow like a dead-pan delivery), "And the master applauded the dishonest steward for acting so astutely. For the worldly are more astute than the other-worldly in dealing with their own kind" (Luke 16:1–8).

Bewildered, $2+2$ says, "Is Jesus condoning dishonesty?" But if the story is allowed to speak with the sparkling indirection of a joke, it says nothing whatever about dishonesty. It commends shrewdness and says, "Just because you're trying to be good, you don't have to go out of your way to be naïve!" Or to put it in proper Gospel language, "Be wary as serpents, innocent as doves" (Matthew 10:16). It may make the further point that if you really want to be innocent in the original sense of the word (that is, "doing no harm"), if you really want to use the things of this world well and faithfully, you will need all the wits you have, used as shrewdly as you know how, in order to accomplish your desire.

Many of Jesus' stories have an unexpected twist to them, an upside-down quality that is typical of jokes. You have to step mighty lively to keep up with them; they'll fool you if you don't watch out. Does the parable of the Good Samaritan (Luke 10:30–37), for instance, directly answer the lawyer's question, "Who is my neighbor?" No— it perpetrates a neat turnabout, like those optical-illusion drawings of staircases that turn themselves inside out and begin going down instead of up as you look at them. The story leads you gently along and then says, "Stop worrying about who is your neighbor. That isn't important. The important thing is to go ahead and *be* a neighbor, as the Samaritan did."

The parable of the laborers in the vineyard (Matthew 20:1–16) is a story that 2+2 has brooded over for centuries. And no wonder, for it annihilates the whole 2+2 concept itself by making the point that there *are* no sums in the Kingdom, there is no "justice" in the tit-for-tat sense. The Kingdom is a gift, and no one is defrauded if, having agreed to work for a reward, he sees someone else getting the same reward for less work.

Then, too, there is the high-class jolter about the king who, having wiped out in one generous gesture the huge debt owed by a servant, later punishes him severely for holding a fellow-servant to a small debt. Pretty vindictive, that king. But as a joke, taken not point by point but for its total impact, the story says nothing whatever about the king. It is talking about the servant; and you are the servant; and the point is that if you have been freed from the 2+2 approach to life you have no business weighing it in on anyone else. In fact, if you do, you show that you were never really free from it in the first place.

Christopher Fry speaks of laughter as "a kind of perception." Jesus, when we put a smile back on his face, calls us to this kind of perception—as far above our usual literal, pedestrian, "serious" outlook as integral calculus is beyond $2 + 2$. And with this perception, these new eyes, he is asking us to see the Kingdom: the state that is beyond our human additions and subtractions; the state—light, joyous, and free, beyond tragedy and retribution—in which the last plays of Shakespeare have their action; the state which children at play enter freely; the state that can be within us as individuals, among us as a group, and all around us as human beings inhabiting God's world—the state in which we shall, when we come to it, stand and say,

> Thou dost show me the path of life;
>   in thy presence there is fulness of joy,
>   in thy right hand are pleasures for evermore.
>   (Psalm 16:11)

6

Jesus as Disturber of the Peace

MANY GREAT LEADERS have felt called upon to be disturbers of the peace.

Socrates was a gadfly to Athenian society.

Jeremiah was an ox-goad to the rulers of Jerusalem.

Luther drove nails into the Church of his time.

Martin Luther King, Jr., stopped the wheels of the Montgomery transportation system.

And Jesus, whom we call the Prince of Peace—where does he stand?

His mother, taking him to the Temple as a baby, is told, "You too shall be pierced to the heart" (Luke 2:35). And later Jesus himself tells his disciples, "You must not think that I have come to bring peace to the earth. I have not come to bring peace, but a sword" (Matthew 10:34).

His first public act is a rebuke to the prevailing values of his time. In the Jewish tradition, baptism was required only of converts, not of the Jews themselves. Yet Jesus, a Jew, receives it at the hands of John, the prophet who calls God's Chosen People a "vipers' brood" and dares to tell them that their hearts and ways need cleansing (Luke 3:7–9).

When the people of his home town first hear Jesus preach and are nodding to one another in surprised approval, he makes a deliberate attempt to upset and annoy them, and succeeds so well that they hustle him out of town and try to kill him (Luke 4:16–29).

His teachings and healings begin to attract attention; something else attracts attention too—the fact that Jesus walks rather casually along the well-marked paths of Jewish law, taking many short cuts and sometimes crashing through a fence or two. He breaks the Sabbath laws, detailed and strict as they are, whenever he sees fit. If his disciples are hungry he allows them to pick grain and eat it as they pass through the fields (Mark 2:23)—and this is work, strictly forbidden by the Sabbath code. If people come to him on the Sabbath for healing, he heals them (Mark 3:1–5; Luke 13:10–14)—work, again. None of this strikes us as very shocking, but we need to remember that the concept of Sabbath rest was as much a cornerstone to the whole Jewish social structure as the concept of private property is to ours. To realize what a social earthquake Jesus' Sabbath actions caused, we have to imagine a man coming into our town, borrowing cars without asking, moving into an empty house, taking cans off the supermarket shelf as he and his friends need them or see someone else needing them. We would call this man a thief; the Jews called Jesus a Sabbath-breaker; and the two accusations are equally serious.

They called him a blasphemer too—the accusation which would ultimately bring about his death. "Blasphemy" is a word without much meaning to us nowadays, but the first episode in the Gospels that calls it forth suggests what it meant to the Jews. Jesus says to a paralyzed man brought to him for healing, "Man, your sins are forgiven." The lawyers and Pharisees standing nearby are horrified: "Who is this fellow with his blasphemous talk? Who but God alone can forgive sins?" (Luke 5:20–21). Man and God occupy separate levels of being, and anyone who shows even the faintest sign of forgetting this fact is a blasphemer.

Sabbath-breaker and blasphemer, Jesus associates with the outcasts of Jewish society (Mark 2:16). He encourages his disciples to pay no attention to the traditional fasts and cleanliness rules (Mark 2:18–20; 7:1–5). He shows none of the respect for family ties that Jewish tradition has always emphasized. When a man, wanting to follow Jesus, says, "Let me go and bury my father first," Jesus replies, "Leave the dead to bury their dead" (Luke 9:59–60). He goes further: "I have come to set a man against his father, a daughter against her mother, a young wife against her mother-in-law; and a man will find his enemies under his own roof" (Matthew 10:35–36). And further still: "If anyone comes to me and does not hate his father and mother, brothers and sisters, even his own life, he cannot be a disciple of mine" (Luke 14:26). Centuries of interpretation have blunted the impact of these sayings, but they were, and are, shocking.

Jesus seldom misses a chance to downgrade respectability. In his parables the pillar-of-society types almost never get a kind word. Priest and Levite alike pass by an injured man on the Jericho road; it is an outcast Samaritan who finally stops to help (Luke 10:30–34). Genuine prayer goes up to God not from the righteous Pharisee, but from the collaborationist tax-gatherer (Luke 18:9–14). And when he addresses them directly, Jesus talks harshly to these respectable people: "I tell you this: tax-gatherers and prostitutes are entering the kingdom of God ahead of you" (Matthew 21:31). "Many, I tell you, will come from east and west to feast with Abraham, Isaac, and Jacob in the kingdom of Heaven. But those who were born to the kingdom will be driven out into the dark, the place of wailing and grinding of teeth" (Matthew 8:11–12).

Questions put to him draw nothing more cooperative than counterquestions, sometimes even counteraccusations. When some Pharisees and lawyers from Jerusalem ask him, "Why do your disciples break the old-established tradition?" he replies, "And what of you? Why do you break God's commandment?" (Matthew 15:1–4). Another group asks him for a sign, to prove to them that he has authority to speak as he does, and he says, "It is a wicked generation that asks for a sign" (Matthew 16:4). Once he even becomes angry with people who question a Sabbath healing (Mark 3:5).

At the height of his power and fame he makes a conspicuous and politically provocative entrance into Jerusalem, during which his disciples shout, "Blessings on him who comes as king in the name of the Lord." And when some Pharisees remonstrate, he replies, "I tell you, if my disciples keep silence, the stones will shout aloud" (Luke 19:38–40).

Immediately afterward he has the audacity to go into the Temple and drive out some authorized dealers who have been doing business there for years (Mark 11:15–16).

Who dares to do such things? And by what right? The Pharisees and lawyers, priests and elders of Jerusalem ask for his credentials. But does a civil question get a civil answer? No—the pin only keeps pricking, the ox-goad digging deeper into the skin. He asks them their opinion on the authority of that other controversial figure, John the Baptist, and when they refuse to commit themselves, says, "Then neither will I tell you by what authority I act" (Mark 11:33). He goes on to undermine their prestige with a series of devastating parables. But when they try to retaliate by asking compromising questions, he can always manage to extricate himself somehow and spring the trap on them instead. And the crowds love him, this terrible man who defies accepted patterns and tries to discredit the people who wish to maintain them.

Demagogue, agitator, revolutionary—he is all these things. The respectable people of his time thought so, and we of the twentieth century, if we read the record honestly, must come to the same conclusion.

He is a disturber of the peace. But why?

To answer this question we have to ask two others.

What is peace?

And what is violence?

The answers are easy, we tell ourselves. Peace is quietness and a steady march of one untroubled day after another, with no problems and crises coming up. And violence, on the other hand, is the breaking up of this happy calm.

But these definitions do not allow for what might be called negative violence, the kind that is exerted by inertia and rigidity. Put your thumb against a dripping faucet. Which is violent, the water which in the end bursts forth, or your thumb, which holds it in to the bursting-point? Close a pot tightly and let it boil awhile. Which is violent, the exploding pressure of the steam which has built up inside, or the enclosing pressure of the lid?

Two images that Jesus used indicate the full scope of the problem of violence. "No one sews a patch of unshrunk cloth on to an old coat; if he does, the patch tears away from it, the new from the old, and leaves a bigger hole. No one puts new wine into old wine-skins; if he does the wine will burst the skins, and then wine and skins are both lost" (Mark 2:21–22). The new cloth will shrink, the new wine will ferment—but is it they who are solely responsible for the disaster—or do old cloth which cannot stretch and the stiff, restraining wineskins have their share in it too?

A social structure can be like the thumb on the faucet, like the old and hardened wineskins. No matter how sound and good a society's basic concepts may be, they can stiffen with age and become a prison as laws grow rigid and practices inhuman. Values can jell into formulas, and the fresh springs of religious insight can freeze into doctrines. A society can dry out like the cracked bed of a desert stream, splitting its people apart into rich and poor, landed and landless, caste and outcast.

Something like this had happened to the Jewish social structure of Jesus' day. As a built-in check to the natural process of aging and hardening, Hebrew law had originally contained the great concept of the Jubilee year (Leviticus 25:10), the fiftieth year during which slaves were freed, property returned to its original owners, and everybody began again. But the Jubilee law remained only a theory; and the process of national hardening, once begun, continued in spite of constant warning from the prophets. "Woe to those who join house to house, who add field to field until there is no more room" (Isaiah 5:8). "Injustice has blossomed, pride has budded. Violence has grown up into a rod of wickedness" (Ezekiel 7:10–11). "From prophet to priest, every one deals falsely. They have healed the wound of my people lightly, saying, 'Peace, peace,' when there is no peace" (Jeremiah 6:13–14).

Such a peace as this is like a rotten orange or a deep abscess, like a tomb covered with whitewash, clean outside but filled with decay inside (Matthew 23:27). Such a peace needs to be disturbed. A society sunk in such a peace must be cut to the heart in order to set its lifeblood flowing again. It must see its laws broken in order to wake up to their deepest meanings. It must feel its traditions challenged in order to affirm the living experience that they perpetuate.

Jesus disturbs the peace of the Temple in Jerusalem in order to open the eyes of the Jews to a far deeper disturbance that has crept in through the years, in order to open their ears to the noise of men bargaining and clinking coins in the spot where once the Temple of Solomon rose in complete silence, like a vision, "with stone prepared at the quarry; so that neither hammer nor axe nor any tool of iron was heard in the temple, while it was being built" (I Kings 6:7).

When Jesus permits his disciples to disregard the laws of cleanliness, he opens the way for teachings about real defilement. The pollution legislated against is only a superficial hint: "A man is not defiled by what goes into his mouth, but by what comes out of it. . . . Wicked thoughts, murder, adultery, fornication, theft, perjury, slander—these all proceed from the heart; and these are the things that defile a man" (Matthew 15:11, 19).

But the Sabbath law, most important of all to the Jews, remains the key to everything. When Jesus allows his hungry disciples to pluck and eat some ears of wheat as they walk through a field one Sabbath day, the Pharisees question him. Can he make them understand?

He tries. First he gives them a precedent out of their tradition: "Have you never read what David did when he and his men were hungry and had nothing to eat? He went into the House of God . . . and ate the consecrated loaves, though no one but a priest is allowed to eat them, and even gave them to his men" (Mark 2:25–26). The whole issue goes much deeper than precedent, however: "The Sabbath was made for the sake of man and not man for the Sabbath" (Mark 2:27). This statement is like an iceberg—nine-tenths of its meaning lies out of sight, implicit in the whole structure of Hebrew law, history, and myth. Why, according to tradition, was the Sabbath made? So that man could rest from his work (Exodus 20:10) as God also rested (Genesis 2:2–3) and as the Hebrew slaves had not been able to do in Egypt (Deuteronomy 5:15). The Sabbath came into being for man's sake, not God's. It is fully as much a merciful answer to man's need as it is an observance owed to God. But food also is a merciful answer to man's need, as it was for David and his men and for the hungry disciples on that Sabbath. Thus, when the Sabbath work rule is broken in order to meet genuine need, it is not broken at all—on the contrary, its truest, deepest meaning is expressed.

Jesus' attitude toward Law as a whole is implied in his answer to the men who ask him what he thinks about the divorce provision in the Mosaic code. "It was because you were so unteachable that he made this rule for you," he comments, and goes on to point out that "in the beginning, at the creation," God made men and women capable of a relationship which is meant to be permanent (Mark 10:5–9). His thought appears to be that laws come into being when men lose their direct insight into what human beings are meant to be and do.

Someone who thinks like this is likely to consider any specific law as secondary to human values, fulfilling its purpose only when it ministers to those values. So Jesus is able to break specific laws on occasion and still to say with complete sincerity and conviction, "Do not suppose that I have come to abolish the Law and the prophets; I did not come to abolish, but to complete" (Matthew 5:17). He is not breaking, he is breaking *through*—through to the underlying laws of human nature and human need.

Similarly, when Jesus challenges the family tie, it is done not to reject or destroy but to enlarge it. Son of God,

Son of Man, he wishes to remind men of greater possibilities of sonship and brotherhood than their daily imagination conceives. "Whoever does the will of my heavenly
Father is my brother, my sister, my mother" (Matthew
12:50). The image itself speaks for Jesus' strong sense of
family, for if he did not value family ties why should he
use them to symbolize the ties he values most? But just as
specific laws can sometimes blind people to the Law of
God and man that lies behind them, so individual family
ties can hold men back from the larger relationship that
Jesus holds out to us—the relationship that has been ours
from the beginning, that of children of God and brothers
to all His other children.

And so Jesus confronts his time, our time, all times, dis-
turbing our peace in order to remind us of our origins. He
questions human society about its actions in order to open
its eyes to their meaning. He asks us to look at what we
have become, to be conscious of how far we have wandered.
He is like a man standing at the mouth of a river, calling
attention to its greasy surface and polluted water—but by
this very act reminding his listeners of the pure clarity of
its source. In word and deed Jesus brings to life the plea
of Amos:

> Let justice roll down like waters,
>   and righteousness like an ever-flowing stream.
>   (Amos 5:24)

And the peace he holds out to us is the genuine peace that
is the fruit of righteousness.

7

Jesus as Antagonist

WHAT DOES JESUS THINK of the people who have allowed their tradition to harden, their society to deteriorate—the spiritual and social leaders, the priests and elders, scribes and Pharisees? Anyone content with the easy generalization that Jesus "hates the sin but loves the sinner" had better take a second look at the man who confronts these men. No, not confronts, attacks—that is the only word.

"Hypocrites—blind fools—snakes—vipers' brood," he calls them.

In a series of parables he compares them to a son who promised his father to go and work in the vineyard but never went; to vine-growers attempting to steal their rented vineyard from its owner; to invited guests too rude to come to their king's feast; to a wedding guest who did not bother to dress up for the occasion (Matthew 21:28– 22:14).

He accuses them of one-upmanship—the art of putting other people down in order to keep yourself up, of shutting other people out in order to keep yourself in. And he says that when they find someone else with the same talent for that art, they train him to be even more rigid and exacting than they are. They pay more attention to finicky surface matters than to basic things. They claim a proud relationship-of-ideals with the dead revolutionaries of the past while they kill every live revolutionary they can find. They are fit for hell; they are whitewashed tombs. (Matthew 23.)

What makes this diatribe all the more shattering is its target; for these are the "good" people, the solid citizens of Jesus' time and the kind of people who are highly esteemed in any era and any culture.

Gentle with prostitutes, drunkards, and collaborationists, with neurotic women and dangerous psychotics, why is Jesus so severe with—well, with us?

For we must face it; these people are ourselves. Where else can we stand in the crowd that gathers round Jesus? We read our Bibles. We respect our laws. We uphold our customs and are hard on people who don't. We are pillars of our society. We go along, comfortably at home in our culture, happily conscious of our righteousness, quietly taking the steps necessary to keep ourselves comfortable and righteous—and occasionally pausing to wonder what evil power makes other men do the things they do.

What's so bad about all that?

Plenty, Jesus seems to think. To him the Pharisees, symbols of this whole syndrome, represent the spirit of religion set in concrete, "goodness" at its stuffiest and worst. Not only are they responsible for what has happened to the world of his time, they *are* what has happened. What they are shouts louder than what they do or say; and what they are is death. If human goodness exists at all, it is something quite different from this pious travesty.

Many Gospel episodes show how Jesus reacts to the Pharisees; one in particular (Matthew 12:22–32) develops and explains it. Jesus has healed a man, generating the aura of power that always surrounds him at such times and stirring up a sense of excitement in the crowd. They respond simply and directly to both person and event, and ask, "Can this be the Messiah?"

The Pharisees, in sharp contrast, do very much what we might find ourselves doing if someone walked into our prevailing religious and social structure, pointed out all its faults and superficialities, and then proceeded to demonstrate real power over a situation that we had been successfully ignoring for years. Suppose—to take an extreme example—a self-styled communist and atheist were to come into our community and do a magnificent job of clearing up a bad slum area: what would we do, what would we say, how would we feel?

The Pharisees sum up their reaction in one sentence of complete condemnation: "It is only by Beelzebub prince of devils that this man drives the devils out." This healing cannot possibly be good; they do not approve of the man who has done it, and to admit that what he does is good would involve them in re-examining some of their basic premises and ways of doing things. They cannot afford to acknowledge the healing, so they condemn it.

Jesus answers their accusation on increasing levels of depth. First, on a purely logical plane, he points out that if evil worked against itself it would destroy itself. Then he appeals to their own experience. "If it is by Beelzebub that I cast out devils, by whom do your own people drive them out? If this is your argument, they themselves will refute you." In other words, "You've seen healings before, and when they are done within your own tradition you recognize that they are good. So how can you say that healing is bad when I do it?"

Is the kind of double-standard thinking that Jesus describes here confined to first-century Palestine? Is, for example, the foreign aid of another nation self-seeking and sinister, while our own is generous and good? If our planes

fly over another nation's boundaries, is it weather recon-
naissance, while their flights over ours are spying? Is a lie
told by a friend white, a truth told by an enemy black with
hypocrisy? Nationally and individually we all do this kind
of thing in greater or less degree.

But if we can stop, if we can take up the generosity and
honesty that will give a good name to a good deed, wherever we find it and whatever violence it does to our cher-
ished concepts of our own rightness and goodness, then—
as Jesus says to the Pharisees—"be sure that the kingdom
of God has already come upon you."

Kingdom of God—that seems like a large state to be
brought about by such small everyday attitudes as consistency, fairness, and open-mindedness. But it is what
Jesus promises; and he goes on to invoke its opposite, the
kingdom of Hell. For there follows a warning, so stern and
solemn that it has frightened many generations of Christians. "I tell you this: no sin, no slander is beyond forgiveness for men, except slander spoken against the Spirit, and
that will not be forgiven. Any man who speaks a word
against the Son of Man will be forgiven; but if anyone
speaks against the Holy Spirit, for him there is no forgiveness, either in this age or in the age to come" (Matthew 12:31–32).

How can this great and unforgivable sin possibly have
any connection with anything as small and all-pervasive
as the tendency the Pharisees have shown—the tendency
we all have—to look at things as we want to, to see what
suits us, to turn our eyes away from what we do not want
to see?

But *is* this a small thing? The whole fabric of truth is
torn when we do it; the whole structure of our inner world
is distorted and with it inevitably the whole structure of
the outer world as well.

One would not expect to find such statements as these confirmed in a laboratory; but recent experiments in the area of perception open up speculation along these same lines. One group of such experiments was performed over a period of years at Princeton University. Dr. Hadley Cantril confronted observers with various types of visual deception in order to find out what the effect would be upon their estimates of relative distance and size. For instance an observer, looking at a tall man and a two-year-old boy standing in the corners of a room which he knew, intellectually, to be distorted, with one corner much smaller than the other (but which was so arranged as to look rectangular from his viewing-point) would nevertheless "see" the room as straight and the boy as taller than the man. Dr. Cantril's explanation for this almost universal result was that our fixed idea of the shape of a room is much stronger than any fixed idea we may have about the size of human beings. Such findings as these confirm what some of us have suspected all along—that in our everyday observation of the world around us we tend to see not necessarily what is there, but what we expect to see, what our experience has conditioned us to see.

Another relevant set of experiments was performed by Dr. Solomon Asch of Swarthmore College. The ostensible purpose was to see how accurately a group could estimate the relative length of two lines by looking at them; actually they were rigged experiments performed on only one member of each group. All the other group members were instructed to give a few correct estimates in the beginning, then make false estimates. The object was to see how long the one member who was trying to see accurately and answer truthfully could hold out against the psychological pressure of everyone else's false answers. An article which described the experiments * was illustrated by pictures of one young man who, all alone, was trying to see and tell the truth—a person under torture, to judge by his expression. Three-quarters of those tested wavered from their goal in various ways and various degrees of seriousness. Some began to say what the group said because, though they were aware that the group was wrong, they could not bear to single themselves out by differing; some capitulated because they began to doubt their own sanity; and a few even claimed that they actually began to see what the group reported.

If this kind of brainwashing can be done to a group of highly intelligent young men, trained to see and think clearly, what about the rest of us? If people can induce false speaking and false seeing in one another over a matter as clear-cut as the relative lengths of two lines, what about other matters not so easy to verify, matters in which popular opinion and the prevailing climate of thought are our chief guides? How much of what we think is so *is* so?

When this last question was put to Dr. Asch, conductor of the experiments, his reply was, "I don't know—maybe twenty per cent. I only wish I knew which twenty per cent!"

Here, pinpointed, is the situation which Jesus warns us against. We might be helping one another, we might all be working together to create a great connective fabric of truth and honesty which would cover all the earth and make out of our human variety a viable whole. But except in the scientific disciplines we have not done so; and therefore we are divided into a cosmic Punch and Judy show, hitting one another over the head with our wishful and partial thought-structures.

* *Scientific American*, Vol. 193, No. 5 (Nov. 1955), pp. 18, 31–35.

The division begins afresh and individually in each one of us with the same moment: the moment when we are confronted by something—an action, a fact, a person, an opinion, a way of life—and make of it what we wish instead of acknowledging the truth that confronts us in it.

In the Gospel of John, the Holy Spirit or Strengthener is defined as "the Spirit of Truth" (John 14:16). The sin of which Jesus accuses the Pharisees, then, is a sin against the power within us by which truth is seen and known and shared. Can any sin be more basic, more far-reaching, or produce more irremediable and long-lasting results? No wonder Jesus says it "will not be forgiven . . . either in this age or in the age to come." He is not so much threatening future external judgment as stating a present internal fact. All other sins carry within them the possibility of repentance—of seeing, even at the moment of committing them, the truth about their destructive and enslaving power over us. And, seeing, we can turn and begin to make our way out of the destruction and slavery. But a sin against truth takes away the very means of repentance. It blinds the eyes by which we see. It leaves us with no way of standing off and seeing the sin for what it is, for its evil is at the center of the soul. For this sin "there is no forgiveness" because while it lasts it cannot be repented of.

"The lamp of your body is the eye. When your eyes are sound, you have light for your whole body; but when the eyes are bad, you are in darkness. See to it then that the light you have is not darkness" (Luke 11:34–35).

This then is Jesus' greatest concern—that the light that is in us be not darkness, that we not twist and turn the truth to suit ourselves, that we "beware of the leaven of the Pharisees, which is hypocrisy" (Luke 12:1, RSV). "Leaven" is a powerful word in this context; for yeast works in dough, imperceptibly and gradually changing its nature, just as the world of human beings is subtly altered when falsehood instead of truth works in it. And hypocrisy is nothing less than the great inward gulf between man and truth that is the sin against the Spirit.

We are already the victims of this sin; to some extent we have all, as Dante said of the occupants of his Hell, "lost the good of intellect." We are all bound in the web that the human race, with its talent for self-interested distortion and rationalization, has woven round the world. Jesus says that there is no forgiveness, ever. Are we not, then, all caught in it permanently?

An important distinction needs to be made here. Jesus is not holding us responsible for the already-woven web we are caught in; he is talking about the moment when we deliberately choose to spin another strand in it—the moment when a truth confronts us in clear and recognizable form and we close our eyes to it. However distorted our total environment may be, however little choice our education and way of life may give us as to what we see in our world and how we interpret it, moments of clarity confront us now and then, and they are within our area of freedom. For these we are responsible; upon them depend our own inner heaven and hell, right now, every minute.

And Jesus, who brings the scribes and Pharisees (and us?) to this moment—what about him? After all, how can he expect them to listen seriously to someone who appears out of nowhere (or Nazareth, which in Jewish tradition is perhaps worse) and starts talking as if he knew all about everything? What gives him the right to challenge them and their ways?

A request for credentials seems reasonable; yet Jesus becomes almost as vehement over it as over the Beelzebub episode. The Pharisees ask him to provide a "sign" which will stamp his mission and his message with heavenly authority, and he replies, "This is a wicked generation. It demands a sign, and the only sign that will be given to it is the sign of Jonah" (Luke 11:29). There is a clue to Jesus' reaction in his use of the Jonah story, for the sign of Jonah was no mighty blaze of power from heaven; it was the fact that when Jonah came and preached the word of God to the people of Nineveh, *they repented* (Luke 11:32). They did not ask who Jonah was and what right he had to preach to them; they responded directly to the truth in what he said, and acted upon it. They were not antagonized by their antagonist; they allowed themselves to be disturbed and they changed their ways.

And so Jesus comes supported only by the truth of what he says. He comes as antagonist, hoping that we will not be antagonized; for he longs to save us from our own pharisaical rightness and righteousness—from that fine score that we add up for ourselves in the ledger we have volunteered to keep for God. Like the Pharisee in the parable we are "good" and we know it; and we pray, "I thank thee, O God, that I am not like the rest of men, greedy, dishonest, adulterous. . . . I fast twice a week; I pay tithes on all that I get" (Luke 18:11). But Jesus wants us to realize that no such ledger exists, for in fact no sum is possible: "no one is good except God alone" (Mark 10:18).

Only when we have stopped the bookkeeping and thrown away the ledger can we receive the gift God wants to give us—a heart truly open to his goodness and mercy, ready for his righteousness. "How blest are those who know that they are poor; the kingdom of Heaven is theirs" (Matthew 5:3).

This is the good news that Jesus, our antagonist and savior, brings to us—Pharisees one and all—if we will listen.

8

Jesus as Conformist

IN THE TWO PRECEDING CHAPTERS we have met Jesus as
a nonconformist; but his attitude toward his environment
is too complex to be summed up under a single heading.
What is the full story of his relation to Law, to convention, to tradition? What about Jesus as conformist—is that
in the picture too?

Many incidents in the Gospels either state or hint at the
extent to which Jesus accepts, or supports, or actively defends the status quo.

When we first meet him in the Gospel of Matthew, he
is resisting John the Baptist's attempt to make a special
case out of him and relax a rule in his favor. "We do well,"
he says, "to conform in this way with all that God requires" (Matthew 3:15). In the desert he bases his resistance to the Tempter solidly on the bedrock of Old Testament Law, quoting almost verbatim from Deuteronomy
8:3, 6:16, and 6:13 (Matthew 4:4, 7, 10).

When a lawyer asks, "Master, what must I do to inherit
eternal life?" Jesus replies, "What is written in the Law?"
(Luke 10:25–26). And when a rich man asks him the same
question, he says, "You know the commandments: 'Do not
murder; do not commit adultery; do not steal; do not give
false witness; do not defraud; honor your father and

mother" (Mark 10:19). In both episodes the legal material
leads into further teaching—to the lawyer about neighbor-
liness, to the rich man about poverty; and in both it is
obvious that he considers the Old Testament Law the
foundation and starting-point for all his thought. Even in
the Sermon on the Mount, where the section on Law is set
up in a "You have heard . . . but I say" contrasting balance, each paragraph makes it clear that the balance is not
Either/Or, but Much/More—a development and (as he
says) a fulfilling or completing of the Law.

Several of the stories and sayings show him upholding
even its fine points. In the Sermon on the Mount he says,
"I tell you this: so long as heaven and earth endure, not
a letter, not a stroke will disappear from the Law until all
that must happen has happened" (Matthew 5:18). He heals
lepers and tells them to report to the priests in accordance
with the minute regulations concerning leprosy laid down
in Leviticus (Mark 1:44). Once he obeys a law that he does
not consider binding: when the collectors of the temple-
tax come around, he first demonstrates to Peter that the
law need not apply to either of them, and then tells him
to pay it anyway, for both of them, because, "we do not
want to cause difficulty for these people" (Matthew 17:24–
27).

He submits to authority, literally to the point of death.
On that night in Gethsemane no external factors hold him
motionless in the path of the senseless destruction that is
advancing upon him and his work. He has the chance to
escape, but he does not take it. Like Socrates at a similar
point of crisis, he accepts the fate that the leaders of his
world have determined for him. Later that night at the
Jewish hearing, when he is standing silent, letting accusations fly around his head and lose themselves in thin air,
the high priest demands of him a direct answer to a direct

question. Jesus obeys, answers—and seals his death (Mark 14:61–62).

His attitude toward convention and custom is unrebellious. While the Gospels describe John the Baptist's strange attire, they say nothing to indicate that Jesus dresses unconventionally; and there is even a hint in the Greek of Matthew 9:20 (but lost in most modern translations) that he wears a fringe on his robe similar to the ones he later scolds the scribes and Pharisees for making too wide and conspicuous (Matthew 23:5). In eating and drinking—unlike John the Baptist again—he takes what comes. He goes to parties in the towns, he eats chunks of bread out on the hills; it is all the same to him. He takes what lodging or lack of it is available, and though in two of the Gospels he says that he has nowhere to lay his head, a third indicates that he establishes a home or headquarters of his own when he needs one (Mark 3:19, RSV). He moves freely in this whole area of life and appears to be guided in it entirely by what convention and circumstance suggest.

His attitude toward the troubled political situation of his time seems to be equally relaxed. The humiliating road-rule of the Roman army that any soldier could compel any member of a subject nation to carry his baggage one mile, he notices only to develop further: "If a man in authority makes you go one mile, go with him two" (Matthew 5:41). When his disciples bring him news of a Roman atrocity, he focuses not on the atrocity but on the Galileans who were victimized, and adds, "Unless you repent, you will all of you come to the same end." Repent? Of what? He goes on to speak about eighteen people who were killed when a tower fell on them at Siloam, and says, "Do you imagine that they were more guilty than all the other people living in Jerusalem? I tell you they were not;

but unless you repent, you will all of you come to the same
end" (Luke 13:1–5). Guilty of what? Repent of what?

We long for the lost news stories behind these headlines.
But one possibility strongly suggests itself. The Romans
were not given to casual atrocities or to interfering with
religious observances, but they pounced on rebellion or
even the hint of it. Had these Galileans "whose blood
Pilate had mixed with their sacrifices" been plotting
against the Empire? A tower in those days, as in the Middle Ages, often served as both military stronghold and jail.
Were these eighteen people revolutionaries held in a jail
which collapsed on them?

If the hypothesis is tenable, these stories hold a strong
hint of Jesus' attitude toward the Roman occupation. He
seems serene in the conviction that it does not conflict with
the Kingdom he wishes to bring in—that the individual
and social state which he calls the Kingdom of God does
not depend upon political structure at all. He seems to be
equally convinced that any policy of militant Jewish na-
tionalism can lead only to destruction. He says to the people of this occupied country, "Why can you not judge for
yourselves what is the right course? While you are going
with your opponent to court, make an effort to settle with
him while you are still on the way; otherwise he may drag
you before the judge, and the judge hand you over to the
constable, and the constable put you in jail. I tell you, you
will not come out until you have paid the last farthing"
(Luke 12:57–59). The Jews paid that last farthing in A.D.
70 when Titus besieged and destroyed Jerusalem as an in-
corrigible center of rebellion.

No—Jesus is not a rebel in the usual sense, or in the
usual areas of politics, dress, and personal behavior. He
evidently does not believe in wasting time and energy on
resistance or dissent over what are for him unimportant

areas of life. On major matters his stand is summed up well in a saying found in a sixth-century manuscript of the Gospel of Luke: "Seeing someone working on the sabbath, he said to him, 'Man, if indeed you know what you are doing, you are blessed; but if you do not know, you are cursed, and a transgressor of the law.' " * Law and tradition are to be broken not lightly, but only after searching thought and out of the knowledge that comes from going deep into the heart of both.

Jesus seems to have in mind no sharp break with the past. He wants to correct his tradition when it has gone astray and he hopes to develop its as-yet-unexplored possibilities, but for the rest he feels himself to be its son; it has supported, nourished, and taught him, and he cherishes it all his life from beginning to end.

He seeks it actively as a boy, when his parents bring him to Jerusalem for the traditional Passover feast and he stays on with the teachers in the Temple, "listening to them and asking them questions" (Luke 2:46, RSV). What he learns from his tradition becomes so much a part of him, so inextricably woven into his consciousness, that there is hardly a single personal experience reported in the Gospels that does not find its source or its mode of expression in the Old Testament writings.

At his Baptism, God's acceptance comes to him in words which fuse together Psalm 2:7 and Isaiah 42:1 into one tremendous statement: "Thou are my Son, my Beloved; on thee my favor rests" (Mark 1:11). Later, in the desert, Satan comes to him straight out of the book of Job, to tempt and test him.

At the Last Supper the traditional Hebrew concepts of covenant and sacrifice blend in his mind with the tradi-

* *Gospel Parallels* (Camden, N.J.: Thomas Nelson & Sons, 1949), p. 51, note. Used by permission.

tional Hebrew feast of the Passover and its sacrificial lamb
to make the symbol of his life and death which he leaves
as his heritage to his disciples.

On the Cross his sense of loss and his basic trust both find
expression through the words of Psalm 22:1, "My God, my
God, why hast thou forsaken me?" (Mark 15:34), and
Psalm 31:5, "Into thy hands I commit my spirit" (Luke
23:46). To be quoting poetry at such a time—it seems psy-
chologically impossible. But not if the poetry has become
so much a part of one that it forms and frames the inner
response to the outer event and gives it its expression, as
it does here.

Jesus' three most central concepts and most important
teachings have their origin in Old Testament thought. The
idea of God as Father comes from there, and so does the
concept of the Kingdom. His two Great Commandments
are from the Old Testament, word for word. This un-
broken line goes right through his teaching; he has hardly
a single thought that does not come in one way or another
from his tradition.

Then what is new about Jesus? Why do we consider
him an original thinker? Why have we accepted him all
these years as a great creative spirit?

"Creative," says John Livingston Lowes,

is one of those hypnotic words which are prone to cast a
spell upon our understanding and dissolve our thinking into
haze. And out of this nebulous state of the intellect springs
a strange but widely prevalent idea. The shaping spirit of
Imagination sits aloof, like God as He is commonly con-
ceived, creating in some thaumaturgic fashion out of nothing its visionary world. That and that only is deemed to be
"originality"—that, and not the imperial moulding of old
matter into imperishably new forms. . . . In the world of the
shaping spirit, save for its patterns, there is nothing new
that was not old. For the work of the creators is the mastery

and transmutation and reordering into shapes of beauty of the given universe within us and without us.*

"The imperial moulding of old matter into imperishably new forms"—there could hardly be a better description of Jesus' way with his tradition. His teachings are not copyings; they grow like flowers from the seeds planted in his mind by the Old Testament.

Moses, speaking of God to the people of Israel, asks, "Is not he your father, who created you?" (Deuteronomy 32:6). A poet makes a simile: "As a father pities his children, so the Lord pities those who fear him" (Psalm 103:13). And a proverb-writer sets forth the other side of the image: "The Lord reproves him whom he loves, as a father the son in whom he delights" (Proverbs 3:12). "Thou, O Lord, art our Father," exclaims one prophet (Isaiah 63:16); and another asks, "Have we not all one father? Has not one God created us?" (Malachi 2:10). In these hints, these signposts pointing all in one direction, the shaping spirit of Jesus discerns the image of God as loving Father and frames the response that He calls forth—the great prayer central to his thought, which begins "Our Father."

When the men of Israel ask Gideon to be their king, he says, "I will not rule over you. . . . The Lord will rule over you" (Judges 8:23). There were judges in Israel until the last one, Samuel, grew old and tired, and the people asked for a king. And when Samuel prayed in sorrow over it, the Lord said to him, "They have not rejected you, but they have rejected me from being king over them" (I Samuel 8:7). It was a mighty concept, this idea of God as king of the nation; and through all the years and the kings both

---

* *The Road to Xanadu* (rev. ed., Boston: Houghton Mifflin Company, 1964), pp. 391, 396. Used by permission.

bad and good, it was submerged but never quite lost. Jesus shapes and develops it into the Kingdom of the Father—a living, growing entity and unity, sustained by and subject to the creative power of God.

Two Old Testament passages, Deuteronomy 6:5 and Leviticus 19:18, come together in his mind and produce the explosion of insight that is the Law of Love (Matthew 22:37–39). In it three relationships—to God, to neighbor, and to self—illuminate one another and among them define and develop the meaning of the word "love" in such a way that it becomes not the large amorphous area of feeling that we tend to think it is, but an attitude that human beings can will to maintain, a Way that they can follow in all their actions and thoughts.

Perhaps it is this "imperial moulding" of the tradition that people sense in Jesus at the moments when it is said of him that he "taught them as one who had authority, and not as the scribes" (Mark 1:22, RSV). Authority, author—the two words are close kin, and the relationship between them suggests the creative power that marks Jesus' shaping work on his tradition. He does not break with or destroy the old; he looks at it with an eye that sees freshly, and brings to bear upon it a mind that makes all things new.

At one point in his teaching he speaks of the impossibility of harmonizing old and new when the old is rigid and the new in a state of ferment. At another point he speaks quite differently of their relationship. It is at the close of some of his most creative work on traditional material, the parable-teaching about the Kingdom.

"Have you grasped all this?" he asks the disciples.

They say, "Yes."

"You can see, then," Jesus continues, "how every one who knows the Law and becomes a disciple of the kingdom of Heaven is like a householder who can produce from his store both the new and the old" (Matthew 13:51–52, Phillips).

In all of Jesus' teaching, in all of his life, there is no complete, despairing break with the past, but a continual turning toward it for its deepest, freshest springs of insight—a continual recognition of the old as the treasure-house out of which the new comes.

9

Jesus as Organizer

IT IS ALMOST IMPOSSIBLE to think of Jesus as in any sense an Organization Man. Yet one of the greatest organizations in history, the Church, claims its origin from him.

What does Jesus think of organizations? Up to now he has appeared primarily as an individual working with individuals, a person standing alone within (and often against) the prevailing social, religious, and political structures of his time. His opinion of them is ambiguous and nowhere flatly stated; but his general attitude seems to be one of distrust. The reason for this distrust is expressed in a single telling image that is part of his denunciation of the Jewish Establishment of his time: "Look, look! there is your temple, forsaken by God" (Matthew 23:38).

As an outward framework takes form, the spirit at its center tends to vanish, leaving nothing behind—not even the awareness that it has gone. Anyone who looks around him can see the constant threat and recurrent danger of this possibility in his club, business, church, city, state, nation: the picture that Jesus sets before us is a timeless one.

But life demands organization, all the way from cells making up a human body to human beings making up a state; all the way from the first news of the Kingdom to the Kingdom itself. The moment of hearing and receiving the Word can be (perhaps must be) a highly private and individual one; but the rest requires organization—organization of the individual's whole life around the truth he has found; of the small group around the spirit they find within and among them; of the whole society around that small group.

Life demands organization; but organizations destroy the central life which first gave them birth. It is one of the terrible paradoxes which give human life its tentative quality, and Jesus knows it well.

He must set up some kind of organization, and he does. "He appointed twelve as his companions, whom he would send out to proclaim the Gospel, with a commission to drive out devils" (Mark 3:14–15).

But what to do? How can he forestall the interior death and destruction that he fears? What are the chief dangers that he must guard against?

The concept of hierarchy comes naturally to human minds, and most organizations are based on it. But Jesus describes the kind of leaders who "like to have places of honor at feasts and the chief seats in synagogues, to be greeted respectfully in the street, and to be addressed as 'rabbi'"; and he tells his disciples never to accept such titles or give them to one another: "You must not be called 'rabbi'; for you have one Rabbi, and you are all brothers. Do not call any man on earth 'father'; for you have one Father, and he is in heaven. Nor must you be called 'teacher'; you have one Teacher, the Messiah" (Matthew 23:6–10).

There are to be no titles; there is to be no hierarchy. This organization is to be a band of brothers, not making comparisons among themselves or creating high places for some of them to occupy, but all pressing on together toward entrance into the Kingdom. Superiority or even

equality are not worth thinking about; it is *likeness* that
counts—likeness with the best that they know. "A disciple
is not above his teacher, but everyone when he is fully
taught will be like his teacher" (Luke 6:40, RSV).

Jesus uses several images to describe the attitude which
must pervade his organization. He speaks of servants waiting on table; of shepherds going out to look for lost sheep;
of harvesters gathering in the sheaves. But the most powerful image of all is one that grows out of the story itself—
that of fishermen and fishers of men (Matthew 4:19).

Why did Jesus choose fishermen for his earliest followers? The question is worth pondering.

Fishermen are used to being cold and wet, to enduring
the pounding of storms and the weight of the hot sun without shelter or protection, to meeting danger head-on. They
work hard for uncertain, unpredictable, and often completely unrewarding results. They wait long hours and
days for nets to fill, for fish to take the hook.

And servants? Their work is never done: "Suppose one
of you has a servant ploughing or minding sheep. When
he comes back from the fields, will the master say, 'Come
along at once and sit down'? Will he not rather say, 'Prepare my supper, buckle your belt, and then wait on me
while I have my meal; you can have yours afterwards'?"
(Luke 17:7–8).

And harvesters (Luke 10:2)? Working in a continual
emergency, watching for wind and rain, they sweat in the
hot sun with no rest in sight until the crops are safely in
the barn.

Centuries of familiarity have robbed these mighty
images of most of their power. But they can still tell us, if
we will listen, that the band of Jesus is for hardy souls
whose happiness does not rest in any kind of ease. "What
did you go out to see? A man dressed in silks and satins?

Surely you must look in palaces for grand clothes and luxury" (Luke 7:25). Jesus' disciples are to have nothing to
do with luxury of any kind, inner or outer. They must
work and wait and be shaken by storms—their only reward
the sight of a soul turning and being saved.

Servants—harvesters—fishermen—together these images
also make the point that Jesus' organization does not exist
for its own sake but for the sake of the work it is set up to
do. And it must never lose sight of this fact. Many an organization, founded in order to do a job, has wound up
with its own continued existence as its sole reason for being. Like the trend toward hierarchy, the trend toward
making ends of means seems to be a natural and recurrent
human failing, an aberration that will develop whenever
it can. How to prevent it?

When the disciples are about to set forth on their own,
going out in pairs "like lambs among wolves" (Luke 10:3),
Jesus gives them some operating instructions that at first
glance seem purely arbitrary. But they are worth a second
look to find what Jesus hopes to forestall by them.

He "instructed them to take nothing for the journey
beyond a stick: no bread, no pack, no money in their
belts," depending on the good fortune of each day for
keeping going (Mark 6:8). This may seem like an ineffi-
cient way to operate; but it is a highly effective way to
keep an organization from sinking under its own weight—
to keep it stripped down and ready for action, free to
move easily, unencumbered by its own machinery, unim-
pressed with its own importance. Its members are doing a
job, and if they do it as they should, food and shelter will
come.

For the disciples bring Good News; and they carry with
them one very valuable commodity—peace: "When you
go into a house, let your first words be, 'Peace to this

house.' If there is a man of peace there, your peace will
rest upon him; if not, it will return and rest upon you"
(Luke 10:6). If with these they cannot make their way,
then the heart is gone out of their organization already;
knapsacks and purses will only blind them to its departure.

Success has dangers, though, and Jesus gives further instructions: "When you are admitted to a house, stay there
until you leave those parts" (Mark 6:10). This is practical
advice—a man can be more effective if he has settled headquarters where he may be found easily. But there is more
to what Jesus is saying than that. You have won over the
city; are you going to stop now and celebrate? Are you going to gad about, sit in the chief place at feasts, and generally get caught up in the folderol of useless pleasantness
that goes with popularity? No—stay put and tend to business. Wining and dining make the heart fat as well as the
body, and soon it will be unable to hear the word of God
which it is supposed to receive and give. Do the job: heal
the sick, and say "The kingdom of God has come close to
you" (Luke 10:9).

Failure has its dangers too. An organization can go bank-
rupt, materially or spiritually, over one failure if it stops
there. Keep moving, Jesus tells the disciples—tell these un-
receptive ones too that the kingdom of God has come close
to them; and then shake the dust of that place off your
feet and go on to the next town (Luke 10:10–11).

If failure intensifies to the point of danger and destruction, they are to go freely into that too, without mental
baggage and equipment. "Make up your minds not to prepare your defense beforehand," Jesus tells them, "because
I myself will give you power of utterance and a wisdom
which no opponent will be able to resist" (Luke 21:14–15).
This is the interior equivalent of that other directive to
carry no pack and no money: they are to hold themselves

completely dependent on what the moment offers in the way of guidance and wisdom. And they are not to fear death; they are to fear nothing but the destruction of their souls (Matthew 10:28).

The total picture is of a loose organization, a kind of spiritual guerrilla army, able to live off the land, acting as a group or in pairs, guided not by laws or lieutenants but by some kind of inner certainty, and held together by—well, by what?

By Jesus, of course. But that answer is not so simple as it seems. Who is he? What is he to them? They live with him; they work for him: it makes a huge difference to them who he is. They are his disciples, who will carry on his work: it makes a huge difference to *him* what he is to them.

We have only to look at our own everyday relationships to make this point come clear. Many a mother would like to be (and is equipped to be) much more to her family than the cook and laundress they see her as and so make of her. Many a father longs to be more than a bill-payer for his children. If a classroom full of students constantly requires discipline from a teacher, he can never really teach; he can only be a disciplinarian. Many a child, not yet knowing who or what he is, finds the answer in the eyes fixed upon him and becomes the scientist or musician or football-player that his family has in mind. Many a couple, marrying in what they think is love, find that what each actually wants the other to be is a punching bag.

The list could be endless; for the fact is that the role we play in life depends as much on others as on ourselves. Each of us longs to give himself to others; but the kind of gift he can make is limited by what the others will receive from him.

Jesus too must live and work within this human situa-

tion. What is he to the disciples? Healer, teacher, revolutionary, king—whatever role they see him in, small or
large, that must be his starting point. It is the self-limitation which he must accept.

And so he asks a question of the disciples, the answer to
which means everything for him and for them. First he
leads up to it with a general question: "Who do men say
that the Son of Man is?" That is easy: a prophet, they
reply. Then he asks the real one: "And you—who do you
say I am?" (Matthew 16:13–15).

Peter replies, "You are the Messiah, the Son of the living God." It is a great breakthrough, a tremendous opening of Peter's mind, as if a blind man should suddenly
see—and fully as much a gift of God. Jesus tells Peter so.
"Simon, son of Jonah, you are favored indeed! You did
not learn that from mortal man; it was revealed to you
by my heavenly Father" (Matthew 16:16–17). Peter has,
for the moment at least, turned from "thinking as men
think" to "thinking as God thinks." He has the keys of the
Kingdom.

For there are no limits to his answer. "Son of the living
God"—all the work of God can be begun and carried
through within that context. All of creation, all of life
open up within it and set Jesus completely free to be to
the disciples everything that he has within himself the
power to be. Peter has been able to see, even if only for
a moment, with the new vision that the new man must
have. It is on this kind of vision and understanding that
Jesus' organization can be centered and based.

But when the group, held together by what it has begun
to see in its leader, loses that leader, what will happen
then? What will keep the new spirit and insight alive in
it and hold it to its moment of vision? What can Jesus give

them that will last beyond his physical presence with them?

There follows one of the most marvelous moments in literature—only the death of Socrates comes anywhere near it—in which we can see as we read, as if it were happening before our eyes, spirit and life being given by one to many.

It is the Passover evening, with all that the occasion signifies to devout Jews: holiness, deliverance, guidance, salvation—the hand of God shaping their lives in fulfillment of his promise. The disciples are with Jesus in a large room, a center of light in the night that surrounds them. They eat the sacrificial lamb, symbol of the one killed long ago as a sign for the Passover angel and as food for the long journey to the Promised Land; and then Jesus gives them a new sacrifice for their salvation, new food for their long interior journey to the Kingdom that he has promised them.

> He took bread, and having said the blessing he broke it and gave it to them, with the words, "Take this; this is my body." Then he took a cup, and having offered thanks to God he gave it to them; and they all drank from it. And he said, "This is my blood of the covenant, shed for many."
>
> (Mark 14:22–24)

In this act he is saying, louder even than the words he uses, "This is I, I myself, that I am giving you. This is my life, my spirit, given to me by the Father. I have given it to you all the time that we have been together, day by day, act by act, precept upon precept, line upon line, here a little and there a little. I have given you myself, and you have my life in you. I am going away, but you will not lose me because you have the spirit in which I live and a sure knowledge of the Father who has sent me. The bread and wine are spirit and life to you whenever you drink them; for they mean me."

They mean life; and they mean oneness too; the early Church knew it well. "When we bless 'the cup of blessing,' is it not a means of sharing in the blood of Christ? When we break the bread, is it not a means of sharing in the body of Christ? Because there is one loaf, we, many as we are, are one body; for it is one loaf of which we all partake" (I Corinthians 10:16–17).

And so Jesus leaves them, held together not by an organizational framework of directives, customs, and layers of leadership, but by the ties of muscle, nerve, brain, and the coursing blood that together make the living unity of an organism. He leaves them with a promise, too—the promise of power that will come on that great beginning morning of Pentecost and touch the waiting group with the finger of God, awakening it to be a living body, the body of Christ, the Church.

We may think of the body of Christ as only a vivid image; but early Church writings testify again and again to the fact that the first Christians knew this living unity not as metaphor but as experience and reality. They did not merely think of themselves as one; they knew and felt themselves to be one—not the organizational *one* of the beehive and the anthill, but a *one* which was a whole new dimension of life and power, illuminated by the gifts of the Spirit—faith, hope, and love—and with Christ as its Head, its mind, its spirit, its personality.

They were not always able to remain within the life of this Body; the early accounts show one falling-away after another. Nor are we able, usually, to do more than glimpse its wholeness from a distance. In Ernest Gordon's account of a prison camp on the River Kwai; in Florence Allshorn's plan for a community; in Teilhard de Chardin's vision of the coming-together of all things in Christ, which he calls the Omega point—in things like these we can see the Body of Christ again; and when we do we know that what Jesus said to it long ago is still true:

"I am with you always, to the end of time" (Matthew 28:20).

10

Jesus as Leader

"WHO'S GOING TO GET US OUT OF THIS MESS WE'RE IN?"
It is a good question, now and always—one that people
have been asking ever since they began gathering in
groups.

The question was never sharper than in Jesus' day. Palestine was then an occupied country, and a restless one,
its people stirred by the memory of their long-standing
Covenant with God: "I . . . will be your God, and you shall
be my people" (Leviticus 26:12). Once they had experienced the fulfillment of this promise, in the great days of
David; and through all the years of frustration, political
bondage, and even exile that followed, they had never forgotten. Some day God's Kingdom would come to them
again, and His Anointed One, the Messiah, would save and
deliver them. Out of their different situations in the long
Hebrew history of calamity, the prophets—Isaiah, Jeremiah, Ezekiel, Micah—had spoken forth this continuing
hope; and the Psalms, the Hebrew songbook, had praised
the coming king.

The worse things became, the higher the hope grew:
surely *now* the Messiah would come to keep God's promise. First-century Palestine, chafing under Roman occupation and feeling all through its social, intellectual, and re-

ligious structure the pressures of an alien way of life and a pagan civilization, was such a focal period of expectation.

The Gospels hint now and then at this situation—so continually explosive that Jesus finds it necessary to warn his disciples: "If anyone says to you, 'Look, here is the Messiah,' or 'There he is,' do not believe it. Impostors will come claiming to be messiahs and prophets, and they will produce great signs and wonders to mislead even God's chosen, if such a thing were possible" (Matthew 24:23-24). During the ministry of John the Baptist, "the people were on the tiptoe of expectation, all wondering about John, whether perhaps he was the Messiah" (Luke 3:15). And when Jesus becomes famous, John himself sends his disciples to ask, "Are you the one who is to come, or are we to expect some other?" (Luke 7:19). Though there seems to have been no certainty what particular person would be the Messiah, it is clear that the Messiah was eagerly expected in the *now* of that first-century tension.

When John's disciples come with their question, Jesus has an answer ready for them. "Go and tell John what you have seen and heard: how the blind recover their sight, the lame walk, the lepers are clean, the deaf hear, the dead are raised to life, the poor are hearing the good news— and happy is the man who does not find me a stumbling-block" (Luke 7:22-23).

What kind of answer is that? The question seems to call for a clear-cut Yes or No; but the only definite thing about this reply is that it flatly refuses to be definite. All it does is raise more questions. Is it an answer at all? And if so, what kind? What does it say, if anything, about Jesus' attitude toward this expectation of a Messiah? Does he consider himself this particular kind of Coming One, the political deliverer whom they expect? Does he consider himself the Messiah at all?

To begin finding answers to these questions—perhaps some of the most important ones that we can ask of the Gospels and their central character—we must go back, as before, to the two great experiences with which the public ministry of Jesus begins—the Baptism and the Temptations.

The Baptism shows us Jesus being told of his sonship to this God of the Covenant, this Ruler of a Chosen People (Mark 1:10–11). If a king has a son, the son also is called to rule, lead, and care for the people of the kingdom: the call to Messiahship is certainly an important part of Jesus' experience at this moment.

In the desert we find him exploring this. What does it mean to be Messiah? It does not mean working primarily for the satisfaction of people's physical needs: "Man cannot live on bread alone." Nor does it mean dazzling them with magical proofs, or taking them along dramatically risky roads to greatness: "You are not to put the Lord your God to the test." Most of all it does not mean assuming temporal, political power, for that is the power of darkness; it belongs to the devil and can be had only by serving him. But "you shall do homage to the Lord your God and worship him alone." (Matthew 4:3–10.)

These choices close off all the customary ways of power. If one cannot gain political domination, how is one to rule? If one cannot use either material or miraculous means of freeing people from bondage and suffering, how are they to be freed? At the moment of call to leadership, there seems no way open to be a leader.

But there is another concept of leadership in the Hebrew tradition, a thread woven inconspicuously through the fabric of the Old Testament and now and then showing its color clearly, as in Isaiah 53 or Psalm 22. It is the idea of greatness and power not as qualities which sit on high, commanding respect and service, but as qualities which sustain, support, and serve. It is the secret of God's greatness and of all the true greatness which stems from Him: "Underneath are the everlasting arms" (Deuteronomy 33:27). This concept is revolutionary in the most literal sense of the word, and human values have not yet done more than begin the complete turning upside down that it demands. "Whoever exalts himself will be humbled; and whoever humbles himself will be exalted" (Matthew 23:12)—we tend to see this as a threat of punishment, but it is not; it is a simple statement of the fact as Jesus saw it.

He put it even more clearly to his disciples. "In the world, kings lord it over their subjects; and those in authority are called their country's 'Benefactors.' Not so with you: on the contrary, the highest among you must bear himself like the youngest, the chief of you like a servant. For who is greater—the one who sits at table or the servant who waits on him? Surely the one who sits at table. Yet here am I among you like a servant" (Luke 22:25–27).

In the light of this saying, the Messiahship as Jesus saw it begins to look very different from the Messiahship of first-century Jewish hope and belief.

What is Jesus to do? How is he to fill the place of the long-expected King without getting caught in the atmosphere of expectation that surrounds it? How is he to keep the false hope from exploding into false realization, into the kind of contentious kingship and violent seizure of power that would only prolong and intensify the struggle at the age-old level of hate and destruction? How is he to remake the concept of Messiahship in the minds of his followers so that they will stop asking him for the deliverance he cannot give and be ready to take the salvation he has to offer?

It seems a challenge too great to accept; and yet he is King, Messiah, Savior, and must not deny the role.

How Jesus meets and handles this continuing crisis is perhaps the clearest demonstration in the Gospels that he is not victim of his fate but master of it, from beginning to end.

To begin with, he puts forward no active claim of Messiahship. Once only in the Synoptic Gospels does he accept the title—when he is formally questioned by the High Priest, "Are you the Messiah?" he replies, "I am." Otherwise he is silent on the point. When people ask him if he is the Messiah, he gives an enigmatic answer. He does not encourage the false concept; but neither does he refuse the title, however much it may mean one thing to him and another to those who are applying it to him. He tries to force his hearers to rethink the whole matter, hoping that they will be willing and able to do so. "Happy is the man who does not find me a stumbling-block"—the man who is not so fixed in his ideas and hopes that he cannot see and be won over to the new Messiah, the King who does not sit on a throne but heals the sick and preaches good news to the poor.

And when he asks the disciples for their own insight in the matter and Peter says, "You are the Messiah," what does he do then? First, he tells them that this insight comes from God, not men. Second, he orders them not to tell anyone: they are not to use the term publicly until experience and thought have fully explained it to them. Then the real work starts: "From that time Jesus began to make it clear to his disciples that he had to go to Jerusalem, and there to suffer much from the elders, chief priests, and lawyers; to be put to death and to be raised again on the third day" (Matthew 16:21). How right Jesus was to caution the disciples to silence is shown by the reaction he meets: "Peter took him by the arm and began to rebuke him: 'Heaven forbid!' he said. 'No, Lord, this shall never happen to you.'" Power and success, not suffering and death, are the royal road of the Messiah. Jesus is used to this kind of thinking: he has met it before, in the desert. And he finds the same origin for it here as he did there: he says to Peter, "Away with you, Satan; you are a stumbling-block to me. You think as men think, not as God thinks" (Matthew 16:22–23).

Peter and the other disciples still have everything to learn about the true use of God's power. And no wonder: of the twelve whom Jesus appointed to be with him, one (nicknamed, ironically and hopefully, "Rock") was eager but impulsive and unstable; two were hot-tempered enough to be nicknamed "Sons of Thunder"; one was a traitor; and one was a member of the Zealot party, a group dedicated to the violent overthrow of Roman power in Palestine. It is amazing that Jesus ever expected them to learn any part of the central truth of life and power. Here as in other matters he must have felt that "to God everything is possible" (Mark 10:27).

And so they all go toward Jerusalem, he with his concept of Messiahship, his disciples with theirs. At the last minute he makes one more attempt to clear their minds. "He went on to tell them a parable, because he was now close to Jerusalem and they thought the reign of God might dawn at any moment" (Luke 19:11). It is easy to imagine what they expected: a mighty blaze of power from heaven; a great uprising of the whole city, which would clear it of outsiders and sinners; the throne of David empty, waiting for their leader—everything falling into place, and God's Kingdom coming at last.

But the story Jesus tells them is nothing like this; it is about a nobleman who went away, entrusting money to his servants to trade with until he came back—the parable from which our word "talented" has come, with its underlying idea of gifts given us which we must use well. As a parable of how and when the Kingdom will come, nothing could be further from the intense expectation of that moment; how close it is to the idea that Jesus holds, the rest of his Kingly Progress will tell.

In this expectant setting, nothing could possibly be more potentially dangerous to Jesus' own intention than the entrance into Jerusalem, the city of the Temple, the center of the Jewish faith, the seat of the kingdom of David in old times. How is Jesus to make a kingly entrance on the one hand—and on the other avoid touching off all the outward train of circumstance that could so easily attend it: war, uprising, violence?

He falls back, as so often, on the Old Testament, acting out a verse from one of the prophets to state his case silently and dramatically. "Rejoice greatly, O daughter of Zion! Shout aloud, O daughter of Jerusalem! Lo, your king comes to you; triumphant and victorious is he, humble and riding on an ass" (Zechariah 9:9). Old Testament kings rode horses to battle; if they came in peace, they came as Jesus did, riding on an ass.

Clearly the message given is received, for there is no violence. The crowd of people who have been accompanying Jesus lay green branches along his path and cry out, "Blessings on him who comes in the name of the Lord! Blessings on the coming kingdom of our father David!" (Mark 11:9–10). And that is all.

But one of the accounts hints at a hope of something that never occurred. "When he came in sight of the city, he wept over it and said, 'If only you had known, on this great day, the way that leads to peace! But no; it is hidden from your sight. For a time will come upon you, when

your enemies will . . . not leave you one stone standing on
another, because you did not recognize God's moment
when it came' " (Luke 19:41–44). Jesus can accomplish
the almost impossible task of making a royal entry into an
occupied city without stirring up violence; but to stir up
a great response to his visitation of peace and healing is
beyond even him, for it must come spontaneously out of
the hearts of his hearers. He can be King only over those
who can hear his good news of peace; but who is hearing
it?

No one, seemingly. The time in Jerusalem is full of tension and argument, sharpening division and increasing
danger. Up to now the question has been whether the
Messiahship as Jesus sees it will be swallowed up in the
concept held by the people who support him; now the
question is whether the whole idea will sink without trace
and his Messiahship be lost forever under the current of
opposition that is beginning to run high.

What is a rejected leader, a lost Savior to do? How is
he to behave? What can he do to save, if not himself, at
least his message, the truth for which he is willing to die?

Surprisingly, Jesus becomes more aggressive, rather than
less. He makes a dramatic statement, couched more in action than words, about the degradation of the Temple in
the busy commercial city that Jerusalem has become. To
all attempts of the religious leaders, first to make him de-
clare himself and then to catch him by trick questions, he
replies by showing up their specious and self-saving line
of thought on all important matters.

He goes still further: he tells them what he thinks of
them in words so strong and devastating as to dispose forever of the "gentle Jesus" image. "Alas, alas for you, lawyers and Pharisees, hypocrites that you are! You shut the
door of the kingdom of Heaven in men's faces; you do not

enter yourselves, and when others are entering, you stop
them. . . . You travel over sea and land to win one con-
vert; and when you have won him you make him twice as
fit for hell as you are yourselves" (Matthew 23:13, 15).

When he is alone with his followers he tries to prepare
them for the hard time to come. There will be false leaders; there will be wars and terrors. The disciples will be
delivered up, tried, and some of them put to death. "Do
not fall into a panic," he tells them. "I myself will give
you power of utterance and a wisdom which no opponent
will be able to resist or refute. . . . By standing firm you
will win true life for yourselves" (Luke 21:9, 15, 19). He
fills their last meal together with all the overtones of deliverance which he is offering to them and the world, the
open door into a new Promised Land of the heart. They
follow him to Gethsemane and—dimly, half-dreaming,
while they are "asleep, worn out by grief" (Luke 22:45)—
are aware of him as he undergoes his own human struggle
with the catastrophe ahead, coming out of it victorious and
ready to endure anything.

He is arrested and brought first before the Jewish leaders, then the Roman governor. The charge in both hear-
ings is the same, though stated differently: in both it hangs
on the question of leadership. "Are you the Messiah?" the
high priest asks (Matthew 26:63): do you claim to be the
Anointed One, God's Chosen King? Pilate asks, "Are you
the king of the Jews?" (Matthew 27:11)—are you a claim-
ant to the throne, a potential threat to Roman power?

The circumstances of the trial are only peripheral: what
is central is Jesus himself. He endures; he stands within
the situation, doing nothing either to aggravate or min-
imize it; he neither defends nor condemns himself. In one
account he replies to the high priest's question, "I am"
(Mark 14:62), affirming his own consciousness of the Mes-

siahship now, when the misunderstanding with which it will be received can mean death only to him, not to the concept. In the other accounts he says, to Jewish and Roman questioner alike, "The words are yours" (Matthew 26:64; 27:11)—continuing his challenging ambiguity to the last.

And so the process continues inevitably, taking him to the moment when he is lifted up in disgrace, alone, with taunting voices down below crying, "Let the Messiah, the king of Israel, come down now from the cross. If we see that, we shall believe" (Mark 15:32). By any ordinary standards, when has a leader ever been more lost? And by any ordinary standards, who could be more lost than the followers of such a leader?

But he is not lost. They are not lost. The hardest part of the Gospel account for us today to understand and accept is what follows: we tend to rebel against the accumulation of incredible detail. But behind all this detail the great facts stand: something happened; somehow these lost followers found their lost leader—not a dream or a ghost or a spiritualized memory, but a living reality.

Into their sadness and defeat and unbelief He comes, giving them insight into His truth and promising them His power—power not to rule and overbear, but to create, sustain, and heal: the newly understood power of the Kingdom of God.

Isaiah had seen the pattern long before—the triumph of the Suffering Servant.

> He shall see the fruit of the travail of his soul and
> be satisfied;
> by his knowledge shall the righteous one, my servant,
> make many to be accounted righteous.
>
> (Isaiah 53:11)

11

Jesus as Revealer

WHAT ARE WE? What is man? No generation in history ever had a more urgent need to know than we. A century of scientific research—with all its discoveries about the operation of muscles, nerves, and brain, the whole psycho-physical relationship—has only served to sharpen the question and make easy answers to it impossible.

And a good thing too; for easy answers are exactly what we do not need. Man is more complex than the most intricate computer, more mysterious than all the still-unsolved mysteries put together.

But we still need an answer—one that will preserve the complexity and mystery, and at the same time give us something to go on.

What is man? The Old Testament has the beginning of an answer. God spoke, and Abraham listened. He called, and Samuel said, "Speak, Lord, for thy servant hears" (I Samuel 3:9). God said to Ezekiel, "Son of man, stand upon your feet, and I will speak with you" (Ezekiel 2:1). Man can stand before God and hear what He says—this is his uniqueness, this is what he was created to do.

St. Francis of Assisi once spent a whole night on his knees in prayer, asking over and over again, "My God, who art thou? And who am I?" He knew that the two questions

are inseparable—that man can know himself only by turning toward God and seeking to know Him.

Man turned toward God—that is man; anything else is
less than man. From this point of view man has been sub-
human or at best (as with the prophets, the saints, and
other great religious leaders) only occasionally human
ever since he first appeared on this earth. All of humanity
has been waiting, and waits, for the man wholly turned
toward God to come to show us what human nature was
meant to be and do.

And he has come, and still comes. Nothing in all the
Gospels is as strong and all-pervading as the impression
they give that their central character is wholly turned
toward God. From the first saying reported of the boy in
the Temple: "Did you not know I was bound to be in my
Father's house?" (Luke 2:49), to the last from the Cross:
"Father, into thy hands I commit my spirit" (Luke 23:46),
everything shows this orientation. Even the terrible, despairing last saying of the Matthew-Mark account—"My
God, my God, why hast thou forsaken me?" (Mark 15:34)
—only emphasizes its completeness.

The same thing is true of Jesus' teaching. Its message
from beginning to end is about the Kingdom of God—the
state (whether interior or exterior) in which the will of
God is heard, and attended to, and done. It is about turning toward God. And those who, hearing it, do turn toward
God are related to Jesus in the fulfilled humanity which
he is demonstrating by his life and teaching. "My mother
and my brothers—they are those who hear the word of God
and act upon it" (Luke 8:21). They are related to him,
and like him they are children of God, sharing with him
in the prayer which begins, "*Our* Father."

Yet it is not so simple as it looks. To turn toward God
may be man's unique privilege and endowment; to turn

away from Him is man's unique and inalienable freedom. The Eden story puts it in a nutshell: Adam was created with that privilege and exercised that freedom, and lost the Paradise made for him—the state of simple and direct contact with God, through which flowed all the happiness and peace that he found within and around him. And we children of Adam can find this same division and sorrow around and within us any time we care to look. Turning from God is our legacy, a basic human trend.

William Law tells the rest of the story in his own eighteenth-century language:

> Now here is opened to us the true reason of the whole process of our Saviour's incarnation, passion, death, resurrection and ascension into heaven; it was because fallen man was to go through all these stages as necessary parts of his return to God; and therefore if man was to go out of this fallen state, there must be a son of this fallen man who, as head and fountain of the whole race, could do all this, could go back through all those gates and so make it possible for all the individuals of human nature, as being born of him, to inherit his conquering nature and follow him through all those passages to eternal life.*

The clear picture that the first three Gospels present is of Jesus as a "son of this fallen man," tempted exactly as we are and subject to the same necessities and laws. In the Temptations, Satan comes to him and tries to plant in his mind expectations of special immunities and powers. "No," Jesus replies in effect, "*It is written*—there are laws laid down for men. They are the laws laid down for me." The physical and psychological laws of human existence seem also to have been laid down for him: he walks and needs rest; he is hungry and eats; he is sometimes tired, impatient, angry, or uncertain of his course, like all the rest

---

* *An Appeal to All That Doubt or Disbelieve the Truths of the Gospel* (London: G. Moreton, 1892–1893), p. 144.

of us. To the day of his death, his "process" (to use William Law's word) seems to have been wholly natural.

And through it he is torn continually, like all the rest of us, by the human tendency to turn from God—torn perhaps more intensely than we because of his more intense awareness of the situation, which we move through like blind men who have never heard of the sense of sight. But Jesus sees; he knows. His time of temptation in the desert; his hours of prayer at the time of his sudden popularity as a healer; his strong reaction when followers call him "good master" or say, "You are the Christ"; the hours in the Garden of Gethsemane—these incidents show such moments of tearing-apart, giving us almost a ringside seat at his fight to find and hold, in each situation, the direct, clear, hearing-and-doing relationship with God's Word and Will that keep him continuously and wholly turned toward God.

Out of this tension comes his certainty of the Cross—the knowledge that being an independent self, the center of the universe, answerable to no one, is so much a part of the human heart that any man who resists it feels (and *must* feel) as if he were killing his own self, dying continually day after day. The Cross was no one-time thing to Jesus. We, watching his process, can see that he met it daily within himself before he came to it finally on the hill outside Jerusalem. Out of this day-by-day experience he says to his followers (and to us), "If anyone wishes to be a follower of mine, he must leave self behind; day after day he must take up his cross, and come with me" (Luke 9:23). This is the small gate that few can find, the narrow road that few can travel.

But it broadens out into the largest state possible to the human mind. Even we, in our sporadic attempts to turn toward God and follow His will and way, get occasional glimpses of His nature, like a mountain-climber suddenly seeing a tremendous view as the clouds around him part for a moment.

Jesus, the man wholly turned toward God, sees this view continuously and clearly, a broad landscape bright in the sun and dappled by clouds. In his teachings he tries by every means at his disposal, through pictures and poetry and question and quotation, to make the nature of God, which is so clear to him, visible to others.

Sometimes it is an Old Testament quotation that he presents for fresh consideration: "Go and learn what that text means, 'I require mercy, not sacrifice'" (Matthew 9:13), the prophet Hosea's glimpse of God's nature as not demanding but giving.

Sometimes it is an analogy from nature: "Love your enemies and pray for your persecutors; only so can you be children of your heavenly Father, who makes his sun rise on good and bad alike, and sends the rain on the honest and the dishonest" (Matthew 5:45)—showing forth God as the creator of a natural world which operates by its own laws and favors nobody, leaving each man free to make of it what he will. What we—all of us together, all through history—have made of this equal world is what distorts it and our lives.

> Time's handiworks by time are haunted,
> And nothing now can separate
> The corn and tares compactly grown. . . .
>
> Yet still from Eden springs the root
> As clean as on the starting-day.*

Even in the middle of the distortion something of the basic freedom can still operate: "If you forgive others the

* Edwin Muir, "One Foot in Eden," from *Collected Poems* (London: Faber and Faber, © Oxford University Press, 1956), p. 46.

wrongs they have done, your heavenly Father will also forgive you; but if you do not forgive others, then the wrongs you have done will not be forgiven by your Father" (Matthew 6:14).

Sometimes Jesus uses an image drawn from human behavior at its soundest and most instinctive. "Is there a man among you who will offer his son a stone when he asks for bread? . . . If you then, bad as you are, know how to give your children what is good for them, how much more will your heavenly Father give good things to those who ask him!" (Matthew 7:9, 11). But the good things of God are always an interior gift—so deeply interior that Jesus uses the strong image of secrecy to describe the event: "When you pray, go into a room by yourself, shut the door, and pray to your Father who is there in the secret place; and your Father who sees what is secret will reward you" (Matthew 6:6).

The Father whom Jesus sees is nothing like the God of popular imagination, sitting high above, manipulating nature to reward and punish, creating dramatic and showy effects to impress His power and His will on human beings: a God who (if we really look into the implications of what we are thinking) is captious, jealous, arbitrary, self-centered—made in our own image, in fact.

But we, when we genuinely turn toward God, find ourselves unable to make Him in our image; instead, we find ourselves being made (as Adam was at the beginning) in God's image. Jesus, the Man wholly turned to God, is wholly made in the image of God (it is his uniqueness that he can allow himself to be; we are more resistant). He is wholly derived from God—and so *is* God.

This Man turned toward God, who is God, is the Risen Christ who, his human process completed, comes back after death to his disciples "because it could not be that death should keep him in its grip" (Acts 2:24). He comes to complete what he has taught them, to fulfill their insights about the nature of man and the nature of God, and the process of turning (repentance, John the Baptist called it) that will re-establish the lost relationship between them.

This then is what man is meant to be—wholly turned toward God, wholly free from the demands and limitations of his own nature because God is ruling it and has made it in His own image. It is as if a radio which had lost contact with a broadcasting station's wave length and was producing only static were to be tuned in to the proper wave length again and begin to do what it was designed to do. "So shall we all at last attain to the unity inherent in our faith and our knowledge of the Son of God—to mature manhood, measured by nothing less than the full stature of Christ" (Ephesians 4:13). Guided by the Man wholly turned toward God, we can attain collectively the unity that is mankind, and individually the derived perfection that is man.

What is man? What is God? The Man wholly turned toward God can answer these questions for us—both at once. By the direction in which he turns, he shows us what man's orientation must be and from where he derives his existence. Turned toward God, he sees and knows what in everyday life is lost to the rest of us; and what he sees, he shows. "My soul doth magnify the Lord"—this is a literal description of the work of such a soul in the world: it takes the God whom we cannot see and makes Him visible. "No one has ever seen God; but God's Only Son, he who is nearest to the Father's heart, he has made him known" (John 1:18). And we, looking at Jesus, find that he is transparent, that through him we can see the creative process, the creative power, the Creator Himself at work.

And so the Risen Christ stands before us—child of man,

Son of God, revealer of the true nature of both—calling us as clearly as on that day by the sea he called the disciples. He asks us to look at him in order to find through him the lost and almost forgotten nature of man turned toward God. He asks us to look through his eyes at the world around us in order to find the Kingdom of God. He asks us to see with his vision the Father who loves us. He says to us, "Happy the eyes that see what you are seeing! I tell you, many prophets and kings wished to see what you now see, yet never saw it; to hear what you hear, yet never heard it" (Luke 10:23-24). And he sends us forth to let our lives reveal what we have seen.

12

Jesus as Stranger

THE CHAPTER HEADINGS could go on and on—Jesus as
This, Jesus as That—for there is no end to the areas of
thought and action that Jesus opens up. As the author of
the Fourth Gospel said in closing: "There is much else
that Jesus did. If it were all to be recorded in detail, I
suppose the whole world would not hold the books that
would be written" (John 21:25). But there is one remain-
ing category that in a sense includes all the others, both
written and unwritten.

In old melodramas there used sometimes to appear a
character called simply The Mysterious Stranger. Jesus is
such a stranger, such a mystery in our lives.

But our age is not attuned to mystery. We live in the
age of fact and think that just as $2 + 2 = 4$, so fact $+$ fact
$=$ truth. We live in the age of the photograph and think
that people can be flattened out on a page and seen exactly
as they really are. We live in the age of scientific discovery
and think that there are—or will be, when all the investi-
gating is done—no mysteries.

Jesus baffles us. We cannot solve his mystery by any of
our modern methods.

The Gospels themselves defeat all our attempts to add
fact to fact. To begin with, they cannot be checked or

supplemented by references to other writings of the period; for other references to Jesus are remarkably few, and either so laconic or so obviously phony as to be no help. And when we turn to the Gospels, we find them neither complete nor consistent among or within themselves, each one made up of material which is fragmentary and composed of many different, unblended elements, and all of them together presenting a picture which contains many contradictions.

No wonder it has been fashionable among twentieth-century students of the Gospels to conclude that the historical Jesus cannot be found in them. No wonder C. S. Lewis remarked, more temperately, that the materials for a full biography of Jesus seem to be lacking.

Fact + fact = truth—we can't get anywhere that way, because hardly a single one of the facts can be established. But perhaps the texts, having refused us the lowest level of verification, offer it to us on another level. Here the scholars, having nearly destroyed us, turn to our help; for some of them hold that while no one single episode or saying can be assumed to be historical, taken all together they point in a direction that is historical, toward a person who existed and whose nature can be discerned.

Taken all together, the Gospels give us not fact upon fact, but a validity that stands behind and beyond all that—the validity of a person and of what he shows forth in his life, thought, and work. By looking not at but through the events we can see the person.

Many of our more literal-minded difficulties with the text fall away as we approach it from this direction—questions, for example, of who could have reported the dialogue in the desert, or how anyone knew what Jesus prayed that night in Gethsemane if the disciples with him were all asleep. It no longer matters vitally whether or not one specific incident "really happened" exactly as reported, for they all point toward a real person. Everyone knows by now that Parson Weems' story of young George and the cherry tree is factually false; but everyone also knows that it shows forth very vividly something that was true of Washington throughout his life.

Some of the Gospel stories about Jesus probably fall into the category of the factually false; others are undoubtedly historical; and still others offer a blend of fact and interpretation so well homogenized that separating the two elements is impossible. We cannot tell which is which; the only certainty we can have is that all the stories, taken together, point toward a real person and indicate what he was like.

So now perhaps (we think in our twentieth-century way) we can get on with our photograph-portrait. But there is a trap in this approach too: somebody has to make the picture. One person may pose the subject with his face squarely toward the camera and a light slanting across it in such a way as to accentuate the strong line of his jaw. Others may want to emphasize the intellectual height of his forehead or the gentle spirituality of his eyes.

The process of posing him and setting the lights began early. The crowds who gathered round him saw him as a healer. Some of them, later, saw him as a political leader. The scribes and Pharisees saw him as a demonic blasphemer of the holy.

And it has continued through the centuries. Some early Christians saw him as a mighty, impassive divinity, immune to earthly suffering. Others saw what some Russian icons present—a thin, wan, sickly being, burdened with the world's mortal illness. In the Middle Ages the fighter Christ led the Crusades. And in the nineteenth century a gentle, reasonable, human Christ smiled to see humanity progressing upward.

And the twentieth century? It is hard for an age to be aware of its own bias. But we have seen enough to suspect that while we are looking at the Gospels, the Gospels are looking right back at us.

Yes—what we see when we look at the Gospels tells us a great deal about what we are inwardly. The famous Rorschach ink-blot psychological tests are built on this principle; and one might almost say that the Gospels represent the greatest and most effective Rorschach blot known to man. For two thousand years all kinds of people and all kinds of cultures have seen in them not what Jesus is, but what they are.

But Jesus can survive even this; for he refuses to sit still in any one pose, and if we are honest with ourselves and with the text, sooner or later our biased portraits will be corrected by a process of balancing-out. The disciples themselves were given such correctives from time to time, as one story shows clearly. It comes near the end of the Gospel narrative. Jesus is with his disciples at the house of Simon the leper when a woman comes in and unexpectedly anoints his head with "a small bottle of fragrant oil, very costly"—a lavish gesture of respect and honor. The disciples (who in several episodes have driven Jesus near to despair by their inability to learn and their inadequate responses to situations) think they have this one in the bag. Jesus has always talked about selling all and giving to the poor, hasn't he? Well, then. So they say indignantly, "Why this waste? It could have been sold for a good sum, and the money given to the poor." But Jesus will not hold even this high-minded pose. By-passing the social theory of human generosity, he responds to its immediate fact. "Why must you make trouble for the woman? It is a fine thing she has done for me" (Matthew 26:6–10).

He remains stubbornly a stranger throughout the Gospels. He gives indirect and mystifying answers to questions about himself; and to assumptions about himself he can give crushing replies on occasion: "Why do you call me good? No one is good except God alone" (Mark 10:18). He will not sit for his portrait. He keeps moving. His face cannot be flattened out into a portrait hanging on a wall; it remains three-dimensional, its expressions changing as if he were alive before us. He stands there, a person, with all the qualities of elusiveness and unpredictability that we find sooner or later in our dealings with any individual; and in his presence we feel to the fullest that frightening intuition we sometimes have that no one can ever really know anyone else. We may refuse to face this intuition, we may try to convince ourselves that it is possible to know Jesus, to delineate him clearly, to nail him down; but we always fail.

They nailed him down once, the Gospels tell us—to the Cross. But even then he eluded their grasp, and their failure flowered out into the mystery of his resurrection. So it is still. He meets us as mystery and he shows us mystery; and he will not let us stop anywhere short of this point.

And we are afraid.

Terror is valid in the face of the *numen*, the mystery of things. It can be like a wood in which one gets lost, or a cloud on which one floats away. But if the wood can be charted, if the cloud can be brought down to earth, the world and all human life in it are freshened and enlarged.

Primitive man was afraid when the *numen* met him in rocks and trees and streams; but he stood still and faced it, and through that meeting the idea of the holy came into the world. Jacob was afraid when mystery met him at the ford of Jabbok, but he wrestled with it; and when the experience was finished he said, "I have seen God face to face" (Genesis 32:30). Moses, Isaiah, Jeremiah—they met the numinous experience and were afraid; but they stood still and listened, and knew that it was God who spoke to them out of it.

We do not need to be afraid, for it is Jesus who meets mystery for us—meets it and turns back from the experience to show us its face.

He meets mystery at the Baptism. It speaks to him with a Father's voice; but then—"immediately," as Mark put it (Mark 1:12, RSV)—he meets mystery again in the desert, and it speaks to him with the voice of the Tempter. And we, reading, realize that the two episodes are halves of one experience, and that the whole story is not so very different from some of our own more everyday ones. When we meet the new, the unknown thing—an experience, an opportunity, a great insight (what George Fox called an "opening"), there is always in it both potential blessing and a potential curse. Our task, like Jesus', is to affirm the one and learn from the other—to refuse destruction and to say to the experience, as Jacob did at the ford, "I will not let you go unless you bless me."

The sense of mystery pervades Jesus' teaching and action throughout the Gospels, blazing up now and then "like the lightning-flash that lights up the earth from end to end" (Luke 17:24). "I have come to set fire to the earth, and how I wish it were already kindled! I have a baptism to undergo, and how hampered I am until the ordeal is over!" (Luke 12:49–50). "I thank thee, Father, Lord of heaven and earth, for hiding these things from the learned and wise, and revealing them to the simple" (Matthew 11:25). "But about that day or that hour no one knows . . . not even the Son; only the Father" (Mark 13:32). Sayings like these point toward the cloud, and lead into the forest, of the *numen.*

Jesus meets mystery at the Transfiguration, and the shine of it upon his face dazzles the disciples who are there. They are given a form and framework for their experience —"This is my Son, my Beloved; listen to him" (Mark 9:7). And they learn that they cannot stay on the mountaintop, within the numinous cloud, but must go back down from the height of insight, down to where the action is and the mistakes are made. There they must live and work—and listen, as God told them on the mountaintop.

And we must listen too to this son of mystery, who has taken up the task and responsibility of showing us the Father—the face of mystery that is turned toward man.

As Paul Tillich says in his book *The New Being:*

> Jesus . . . could have become an idol, a national and re-
> ligious hero, fascinating and destructive. This is what the
> disciples and the masses wanted Him to be. They saw Him,
> they loved Him, they saw with and through Him the good
> and the true, the holy itself. But they succumbed to the
> temptation of seeing. They kept to that which must be sac-
> rificed if God shall be seen with and through any mortal
> being. And when He sacrificed Himself they looked away in
> despair, like those whose image and idol is destroyed. But
> He was too strong. He drew their eyes back to Him, but
> now to Him crucified. And they could stand it, for they saw
> with Him and through Him the God who is really God. . . .
> We are not asked to stare at Him, as some do. . . . We are
> not asked to look away from everything but Him, as some
> do. . . . We are not asked to refuse union with what we see,
> as some do. . . . But we are asked to see with and through
> everything into the depth into which He shows the way.*

Jesus begins some of his closest work with the disciples at this point of depth and mystery. "To you," he says, "the

* *The New Being* (New York: Charles Scribner's Sons, 1955), p. 133. Used by permission.

secret of the kingdom of God has been given" (Mark 4:11). The Greek word of the original text is "mystery." It is one of the few New Testament words which have come over directly into English, carrying with them the whole connotation of their use and meaning in the early life of the Christian community. The noun is related to a Greek verb meaning "to be shut" and is a very distant cousin, again through the Greek, of our word "mute."

A "mystery" may be "secret" not because someone chooses to make it one, but because it is incommunicable or very nearly so. Perhaps this whole area of mystery is a silent one where, however hard we try, words will not help us.

But if that is so, why does Jesus talk about it at all? Some of the great religions of the world—notably Buddhism—have set as their firm foundation an absolute refusal to use words about the area of mystery. Buddhist scriptures tell stories of teachers pointing silently at the moon rising or a flower nodding on its stalk. The mystery is left mute, and the pointing finger says directly and wordlessly, "Do you see? Then see!"

Jesus is not silent. He calls out to the crowd, "Listen!" and paints a word-picture of a man walking along with a sack of good seed, sowing it broadcast on fertile soil and rocky ground alike. Then he says in words what the pointing finger says in pantomime: "If you have ears, then hear" (Luke 8:8). When he is alone with the disciples he adds a caution about the use and misuse of talk in this area of mystery: "Take care, then, how you listen" (Luke 8:18). If they receive what he says as an intellectual proposition and try to sort it out objectively in their heads, they will lose it. They must receive it as good seed and let it grow in their hearts.

Mystery calls for response. A medieval mystic once said

of God, "By love may he be gotten and holden, but by the understanding never." At the heart of Jesus' teaching lies the demand for this same response: "Love the Lord your God with all your heart, with all your soul, with all your mind, and with all your strength" (Mark 12:30).

And he adds, "Love your neighbor as yourself." For he does not bring us face to face with the numinous experience as it stood before primitive man, large, amorphous, and threatening. He brings us mystery as something we can found our home on—as relationship, as the Kingdom of God.

"Kingdom" is a cold word for us children of the American Revolution; but perhaps we can warm it up enough to see what it means here. It is the good growth-ground, clean and well kept, in which God's creative process can take place—in which individuals become their richest selves, and their loving relationship with one another and with their King, the Lord their God, can flower out into something greater still, the consummate, organic whole that is imaged in Dante's Mystic Rose at the close of the *Paradiso*.

The first group of Jesus' parables of the Kingdom (Matthew 13:4–52) cluster, for the most part, around the image of growth and point toward the inward power of the seed, which lies dormant when it must, but grows the instant it can—the power whose magnificent explosiveness we fail to notice only because it works gradually.

The key text for this aspect of the Kingdom is "In fact the kingdom of God is among you" (Luke 17:21). "Among you"—"within you"—"in the midst of you"—the Greek phrase has been translated in all three ways.

The process of that minute but mighty power which is symbolized by the seed takes place *within* us—in the inward world that is the sum of all that we have seen and done and experienced and thought. Working there, it redeems the past and shapes the present, making new beings of us fit for its own future.

The process takes place *among* us—in the spirit that guides our life together. Working there it raises our social valleys, levels our social hills, and makes a way for the Lord. It brings about miracles to match the one that took place in that grassy spot where there were plenty of loaves and fishes for everyone. Where it operates freely, it recreates society, and all the things that Jesus said come literally true; there is no need to be anxious about food or drink or clothes. "Set your mind on God's kingdom and his justice before everything else, and all the rest will come to you as well" (Matthew 6:33).

The process takes place *in the midst of* us—in the creative and redemptive power that surrounds us every minute of our lives like the air we breathe without being aware of it. "The kingdom of the Father is spread upon the earth and men do not see it." *

All right—so it is here and now. Then why is the world not perfect and redeemed right this minute? Why are we not the new beings that this teaching promises, right here, right now? All our experience tells us that we are separated from the Kingdom, from this area of growth and life. What about the gap we know and feel?

Jesus gives us no direct answer; but again his finger points. His second group of Kingdom parables (Matthew 21:33–41; 24:43–25:46) cluster around a new image, that of absence; and the question with which they deal might be worded in the symbolic language of the parables themselves, "What to do when the master is away?"

First of all, we must never forget that though the mas-

* *The Gospel According to Thomas*, ed. H. C. Puech *et al.* (New York: Harper & Row, Publishers, 1959), logion 113, p. 57.

ter is absent, he is still the master. We are only stewards of all that we think we own; we are only tenants of this life that we live as if it were ours forever. We are to remember this; and in all that we do we are to hold a certain attitude toward the absent reality of the King and His Kingdom.

To describe this attitude Jesus uses a homely, everyday image: *Wake up!* We are to be as alert as a man is who suspects that his house may be robbed, as wide-awake as a doorman hired to be on the job all night. While living within one set of circumstances, we are to hold ourselves constantly attentive to another—an absent—influence, alive to hints of its presence and alert for its possible coming.

And after all, what is absence? And what is presence? Who is more present to us—someone standing beside us to whom we pay no attention at all, or an absent person on whom all our thoughts are riveted? In calling us to the Kingdom, Jesus calls us to the experience of separated lovers, and tells us that in loving the Kingdom we shall find it close to us, and that when it comes outwardly we shall know that it has been with us all along. When the King comes, we shall say in wonder, "Lord, when was it that we saw you hungry and fed you, or thirsty and gave you drink, a stranger and took you home, or naked and clothed you?" And the King will answer, "I tell you this: anything you did for one of my brothers here . . . you did for me" (Matthew 25:37-40).

Jesus brings us into the mystery of the Kingdom, which was, and is, and shall be; absence and presence are all the same in it, and so are becoming and being. When it is completed, fulfilled, it will show itself for what it is and what we cannot see—a seamless whole, one in all its manifestations. One from the seed through the growing plant to the harvest; one from the invitation through the preparation to the feast; one from the first sight of the beloved through the growth of love to the wedding. Harvest—feast —wedding—Jesus' images of it are all images of fulfillment and rejoicing. And he makes it ours; he gives it to us—not the terrifying, numinous mystery which may destroy us, but the mystery of the Father's Kingdom, in which we can live and move and have our being.